ANIMALS IN
NEWCASTLE

AN ILLUSTRATED HISTORY

ANIMALS IN
NEWCASTLE

AN ILLUSTRATED HISTORY

WENDY PRAHMS

TEMPUS

Frontispiece: The Side in 1820, with bull running loose.

First published 2008

Tempus Publishing
Cirencester Road, Chalford,
Stroud, Gloucestershire, GL6 8PE
www.thehistorypress.co.uk

Tempus Publishing is an imprint of The History Press Ltd

British Library Cataloguing in Publication Data.
A catalogue record for this book is available from the British Library.

ISBN 978 0 7524 4726 1

Typesetting and origination by The History Press Ltd
Printed in Great Britain

Contents

Acknowledgements

Unless otherwise indicated, all pictures are courtesy of Newcastle City Library Local Studies Archives. The author would like to thank the Archives staff for their invaluable help in preparing this book.

About this Book

Animals have been the companions of mankind for thousands of years. Some of them we eat; some were once the main source of heavy labour, pulling coaches, wagons and ploughs; some we saddled and rode. Others, such as racehorses, greyhounds and racing pigeons, provided us with entertainment and still do. Still others lived, and live, with people as pets.

The prosperous city of Newcastle upon Tyne is no different from the rest of the United Kingdom with regard to its use of animals. But as to the *welfare* of animals, it seems that, from the mid-nineteenth century, Newcastle compares rather well with other places. The Royal Society for the Prevention of Cruelty to Animals opened its Newcastle branch in 1873 and its first annual report started by saying that Newcastle had no reputation for misuse of animals. Furthermore, the Newcastle RSPCA was not the only local body interested in animal welfare. In the late nineteenth century the *Chronicle* newspaper launched its Dicky Bird Society for children, the aim being to persuade children, especially bird's-nesting boys, to have more consideration for birds and animals. A decade later Newcastle Dog and Cat Shelter opened and from that date played a major part in the welfare of the city's dogs and cats. The town council itself, which became the city council in 1882, showed concern for animals, especially dairy cows. This book will look in detail at the relevant council minutes, as well as the archives of the Dicky Bird Society and such RSPCA annual reports as were available for my research. These were for the years 1873-83, 1938, and a few others from 1969 onwards. Other sources will be referred to, particularly the archives of the *Chronicle* and reports of relevant debates in Parliament.

This is not simply a book about welfare organisations; still less does it deal with philosophical questions of animal rights. Rather it treats the general interaction of man and animals in Newcastle during the 150 years between 1800 and 1950, although earlier and later dates will be found here as well. Some anecdotes dating from decades later than 1950 are included because these often shed a clear if oblique light on prevailing attitudes. I did not, however, attempt to bring the account up to date. There seemed little point in reiterating stories well within most people's memories. Other pieces of what was news at the time are in because of unusual interest. For instance, it is perhaps not generally known that the world's first dog show took place in this city. Equally surprising, to me at any rate, was the fact that some livestock were being traded between Newcastle and Iceland via barter – involving no money – not much more than a century in the past.

No book about Newcastle and its animals could be complete without considering pit ponies: we shall examine their lives and see how they were the subject of a small scandal in the 1870s.

Horses are dealt with at length since they were the only means of overland transport until the spread of the railways. A long chapter is devoted to livestock for the obvious reason that such animals were used for food and clothes. This chapter necessarily includes a paragraph – under a separate heading – on slaughter: it would have been dishonest to omit this. But horrors are not dwelt upon and readers who wish to know nothing about this aspect of food animals can skip the section. There is also a section on blood sports. This too may strike some readers as gruesome, but it must be remembered that the distaste now generally felt for blood sports is comparatively modern, as indeed is disapproval of cruelty itself, even towards humans. A law still in operation in the nineteenth century covering the treatment of apprentices by their masters had to draw a distinction between correction and cruelty; from this we may surmise that in earlier centuries the distinction had been blurred. As to cruelty to *animals,* the Enlightenment did little to displace the old Christian view that animals were there simply for humans to do with as they liked. For centuries, the Catholic Church taught that a man who starved his dog to death was guilty of no sin. Certainly, in the early nineteenth century blood sports were regarded as part of everyday life; however, equally certainly there were voices raised against them, notably in Parliament.

Also in the book are sections on other animal sports like horse racing (always very popular in Newcastle) and pigeon fancying. There is one chapter on the progress of animal-welfare legislation over the 150 years covered and another on the arguments presented in Parliament and elsewhere during the nineteenth century on the subject of man's duty to animals.

It might be argued that the history of Newcastle's treatment of its animals is not markedly different from that of other English towns: perhaps not, but local developments are always interesting, I would maintain. The unfolding of new laws, bye-laws and customs is more vivid if one can look back at them happening in a familiar place. Besides, Newcastle is my city and I love it, although I am not a native.

Some of the sources of the book have been mentioned already; all are listed at the end. I would have liked to have had a whole unbroken series of Newcastle RSPCA annual reports, but these proved unavailable despite my best efforts. The history of the PDSA was taken from the organisation's own website. Information on pigeon racing in the North East was found in Martin Johnes' article, 'Pigeon Racing and Working-Class Culture in Britain, 1870-1950'. Nineteenth-century cattle-market reports provided information on livestock health while various government publications and books of local history supplied other items.

I have at times taken issue with a view of nineteenth-century animal-welfare measures expressed trenchantly in Harriet Ritvo's book, *The Animal Estate.* Ritvo tries to show that such measures were a covert attempt at social control of the lower classes by the upper. The evidence I saw did not support this view. The upper classes certainly fought to have their own pleasures and practices exempted from the new laws and, to some extent, they were successful (and still are today). But, however they may have fought to keep their sports legal, when laws *were* eventually passed they applied to all classes of society.

Although this book does not attempt to examine the philosophy behind animal-welfare measures, I had better say here that my position is roughly the same as that of the RSPCA: namely that it is permissible for humans to use animals for various human ends but not permissible to misuse them, causing unnecessary suffering. Of course, the words 'misuse' and 'unnecessary' open a whole field of debate: this book's chapter on the arguments in Parliament outlines some of the contending points of view.

I have included many anecdotes and will start with one from the late eighteenth century recorded in a history of Newcastle published in 1789. At that time, Newcastle's town hall had a steeple, like a church, and atop the steeple a weathervane, constructed to turn as the wind changed. One spring, a pair of crows built their nest on this weathervane. People who noticed it thought that the nest would blow down at the first change of wind, or that any eggs laid there would be toppled out. Even if any chick hatched, it could surely not survive in such a precarious roost, they said. However, the crows not only hatched several young; they reared them too.

The next year the same pair of birds returned to the weathervane and started to build again. Alas, other crows, for mysterious reasons of their own, took a dislike to the growing nest and pulled it to pieces. But the following year the determined pair rebuilt the nest, this time without harassment. Again, they reared a brood of chicks; once again, they were fledged in time and flew the nest. For several subsequent years the crows chose the same high and dangerous site for their eggs, though every time the wind changed the nest swung around with the weathervane. It never fell.

Dogs

Newcastle people, like most of the English, have always been dog lovers. Portraits of some of the local aristocracy show them with their dogs; it is notable that as soon as photography became popular, pictures of other classes of people often included their dogs too. One in this book shows a father and his children with their pet Bedlington terrier, the Bedlington being a local breed.

However, dogs, as well as being faithful and loving, can sometimes be a public nuisance or downright dangerous. In the 1890s dogs were forbidden in the newly-created public parks of Newcastle; this was to make it easier to round up the many strays in the city. But the ban led to difficulties: a retired army colonel who sat on the city council complained in a meeting that he could not stop his dog following him through Leazes Park as he set out each morning. Another council member, Mr Heald, said he had been almost arrested for carrying a poodle under his arm through Heaton Park!

Strays were a constant problem: the council minutes for the nineteenth century referred to this repeatedly. Perhaps the great number of strays resulted from the introduction of dog licences (which will be examined later) which meant poor people could no longer afford to keep their dogs. Once homeless, the dogs would form packs and start to breed. The great danger was rabies; cases still occurred from time to time in the UK and in towns dogs were the most usual source of infection. Actual cases of rabies in Newcastle were reported in the council minutes. In 1874 they noted 'two or three mad dogs, found at large in the streets', one of which had bitten a twelve-year-old girl. The poor child later died of hydrophobia, 'after very great suffering'. The following year another, younger child died after a bite from a rabid dog. The city fathers passed draconian measures to deal with these dangerous dogs. In 1883, the *Chronicle* reported a court case concerning a dog which had been killed by the council's dog-catcher without the owner's consent because it was suspected of having rabies. The owner was granted damages.

Boys were not above using their dogs for questionable ends. Time and again the RSPCA annual reports and the council minutes complained of boys setting their dogs on the cattle and sheep at livestock markets. And, of course, the gentry used their dogs for blood sports. On a happier note, greyhound racing became popular during the twentieth century: we will look at some stories from Newcastle's Brough Stadium later.

It was a field-sporting gentleman who brought about Newcastle's claim to fame with regard to dogs. Mr William Rochester Pape of Amble, Northumberland, was first and foremost a sporting gun-maker with his own premises in Newcastle, but from youth he had been interested in gun dogs and bred them as a hobby. His black pointers were famous and widely exported.

Family with Bedlington terrier, 1912.

Frederick, Earl of Carlisle with dog. (courtesy of
Mary Evans Picture Library)

Middle-class family with pet dogs, *c.* 1910.

Prosperous working-class family with terrier.
(courtesy of Mary Evans Picture Library)

Duchess of Newcastle with hunting dog. (courtesy of Mary Evans Picture Library)

Duchess of Newcastle with hunting dogs, *c.* 1920. (courtesy of Mary Evans Picture Library)

In 1859 he organised a dog show at Newcastle Corn Exchange which was the first in the world. It was for two breeds only – pointers and setters – and for male dogs only, no bitches. The pointer class attracted twenty-three entries, the setter class thirty-six, and the show was judged by the editor of *The Field*. The prizes were guns made by Pape himself, valued at fifteen guineas each. Fourteen years later, the National Kennel Club was inaugurated and its first stud book, containing all that was known of authenticated pedigrees, dated back to the Pape dog show.

The following year it was proposed to the council to hold a second dog show, but the vote went against it. People claimed that the first show had made the floor of the Corn Exchange wet and messy for days afterwards, interfering with normal trade and making a bad smell. Others argued however that the smell came from the disinfectant used to clean the floor, not from the dogs' natural functions! William Pape housed his own dogs in beautifully-built stone kennels with central heating (!) at his country home, Coquet Lodge near Warkworth.

Perhaps Newcastle's most noteworthy dog in earlier centuries was not a native but a visitor. In 1754 an exhibition visiting the town featured, among other curiosities, the 'Learned Dog'. According to its showman this dog could 'read, write, and cast accounts, answer various questions on Ovid's *Metamorphoses*, Geography, Roman, English and Sacred History', and knew 'the Greek alphabet &c. &c.' and also 'impenetrable science'. Allegedly he told 'everybody's thoughts in company' and could distinguish 'all sorts of colours'! We know now that such animal prodigies are indeed clever, in that they pick up tiny indiscernible clues from their handlers.

In 1867 Queen Victoria's government introduced dog licences, with the penalty for owning an unlicensed dog set at 5s, a considerable sum for the time, perhaps equivalent to £50 nowadays.

Gypsy boy with dog. (courtesy of Mary Evans Picture Library)

By the end of the century, the fine had risen to 7s 6d. The high charges were intended to deter frivolous and unheeding dog ownership, but they must also have prevented many kind but poor people from owning dogs. Such people might occasionally have a dog licence paid for them by a benefactor who also loved dogs. But many dogs must have been turned out of their homes. In 1883 Newcastle opened its first Lost Dogs' Home and in 1895 Newcastle Cat and Dog Shelter was established. Other animal shelters – official and unofficial – opened over the next few decades. Not all of them lasted long but the fact that they existed at all shows how warmly most people felt about dogs.

Family and pet dog bathing, *c.* 1930.

Only dogs over six months old needed to be licensed – an exemption which took account of the high mortality among puppies. Later legislation covered both harm to dogs and harm caused by dogs. Laws passed in the 1870s and '80s made dog owners liable for injuries caused by dogs to cattle and sheep; later laws dealt with injuries caused to people.

Most dogs in Newcastle in the past, as at present, were kept as pets and there is evidence that their owners thought highly of them. The *Chronicle* had a 'Lost and Found Dogs' column in almost every issue in the mid-nineteenth century, often with rewards offered. In 1858 someone advertised finding 'a small Cocker bitch' which the owner could claim upon 'payment of the cost of this advertisement'.

Some town dogs though were not kept as pets. In the last decades of the nineteenth century and the early ones of the twentieth, dogs were still popular as entertainers, as were other animals. As late as 1958, performing dogs were still drawing audiences at Newcastle Empire.

Something which began in 1958 was the *Chronicle's* children's dog show in Exhibition Park; this became an annual event. The show in 1960 had among its entrants a 3.75lb chihuahua and a 140lb St Bernard! Another dog of the same giant breed which lived at Newcastle Dog and Cat Shelter was offered by the shelter to 'any good owner'. Prospective buyers were warned that the dog ate '2 cow heels, 2lb of meat and meal, and 2lb of dog biscuits per day'! News of the dog travelled throughout the country and he was eventually taken on by someone in Hampshire. The dog's journey to London did not start happily: he was perforce chained in the guard's van where he barked and growled and eventually snapped his chain. After that, he was moved to a second-class carriage which he had to himself.

The 1950s saw the formation of several dog clubs in the city, for instance the Tyne, Wear and Tees boxer dog club. There were even canine training classes every Thursday evening at the Labour Hall in Percy Street. At the end of the decade came a sudden craze for owning whippets. These small-sized greyhounds had previously been looked down on as miners' dogs; now, however, it became smart to own one. The 1959 Newcastle and District Canine Society dog show was won by a whippet, Samarkand's Suncharger.

In 1959, a famous Newcastle dog was put to sleep as a mercy measure by the PDSA. She was a mongrel bitch named Titch and she was eighteen years old. The PDSA had awarded her the Dickin Medal, which is the animals' Victoria Cross for bravery and fidelity in wartime. From 1941-5, throughout the campaigns of Africa and Italy, she had served with the King's Royal Rifle Corps. She had been wounded five times in her life.

The great popularity of dogs during these years reveals, accidentally, an interesting fact: it was perfectly acceptable to call black dogs and cats by the same abusive name that's been used to refer to black people. The word has been taboo for so long now it is hard to imagine people

Young man, possibly a farm worker, with dog. (courtesy of Mary Evans Picture Library)

Tea party with pet spaniels, *c.* 1900.

two generations back casually using it for their pets. Another revelation is the state of mind of some would-be dog owners, one still prevalent in some quarters, I suspect. A scrap-metal dealer in Benton let it be known that he was looking for guard dogs, 'so fierce that their owner wouldn't go near them for a pension'. One wonders how he proposed training them.

In the 1950s and '60s the number of stray dogs increased hugely due to slum clearance. The new flats and houses to which people moved often did not allow dogs (or cats either). So the unwanted pets were either just turned loose or taken to an animal clinic to be put to sleep. Loose dogs caused a lot of traffic accidents. Some were 'temporary' strays turned out whilst their families were on holiday. New boarding kennels opened up to meet the need, but not everyone was willing to pay the fees. The boarding kennels themselves were sometimes seen as a nuisance. Residents of Ponteland in 1959 complained about the constant barking of dogs in the local animal sanctuary. It was suggested that a hedge of thick trees be planted as a baffle for the noise.

The early 1960s saw some 'character' dogs making it into the news. An Alsatian had taken to lying in the middle of the road where Streatfield Grove crossed Wingrove Avenue. Knowing he was there, drivers went carefully and pedestrians crossed warily! One resident described him as being 'as good as a traffic policeman'. A boxer bitch belonging to a hairdresser became a great pet of staff and customers at the salon. What she liked best was to get into chairs under the hairdryers once they had been vacated. A miniature poodle belonging to a family in Cochrane Park could 'sing in key' to a mouth organ or zither. The growing popularity of Alsatians had an unfortunate result: a lot of people got bitten even though the dogs' owners invariably described them as 'soft'.

Demands were made in 1962 for private boarding kennels to be registered; inspectors had described some of them as 'Belsen-like'. The fact that accommodation for dogs could be compared with such a shocking establishment as Belsen shows how far general human compassion for animals had come. True, Mr William Pape a century earlier had housed his dogs in centrally-heated kennels, but he was exceptional. Grand ladies' lapdogs had always lived in unhealthy luxury and so had some of the aristocracy's favourites, but many dogs in eighteenth- and nineteenth-century Britain were kept outdoors in Spartan conditions. Even today, the RSPCA cannot prosecute for cruelty if a dog is kept permanently outdoors, so long as it has shelter of some sort from the worst weather.

Duchess of Cleveland with lapdog. (courtesy of Mary Evans Picture Library)

Cats

Throughout the Middle Ages, cats in Europe were treated with a mixture of gratitude and suspicion – gratitude for keeping rats and mice out of the corn-stores, suspicion because they were believed to be the 'familiars' of witches. Their presence was tolerated but they were not fed since, after all, they were there to kill mice. As belief in witches slowly died out, so did suspicion of cats. Of course, even in the superstitious centuries, some cats had been loved and cared for, notably by the old ladies persecuted as witches. By the mid-1800s pet cats were common, but they were still considered fair game for boys' catapult practice and other torments. The chapter on the Dicky Bird Society shows how prevalent this cruel treatment was. But gradually attitudes changed.

Newcastle RSPCA opened in 1873 and Newcastle Dog and Cat Shelter in 1895. Both took on the protection of cats as well as other animals. Then in the twentieth century, probably the 1940s, came the Newcastle branch of the Cats' Protection League at South Shields. All of these bodies concerned themselves as much with preventing the unchecked breeding of kittens as with caring for living cats and also, dealing humanely with feral cats. During post-war reconstruction and the slum clearance of the 1950s and '60s, great numbers of cats became homeless and some of them turned feral. In 1958 Newcastle RSPCA reported how they had had to put down 3,000 cats every year, mostly as a result of slum clearance in Gateshead. All the organisations for cats' welfare had, and still have, their work cut out dealing with unwanted kittens and all stress the need to have adult pet cats neutered. Nowadays they have, as some have always had, re-homing centres for cats whose owners have died or who cannot care for them. Newcastle RSPCA and PDSA have always had veterinary clinics and boarding facilities for cats. At present the Cats' Protection League, run entirely by volunteers, has twenty-nine adoption centres countrywide and its National Cat Centre combines cat adoption, public education and veterinary care. Of all the organisations, only the RSPCA has, and has always had, the legal power to bring prosecutions for cruelty: a power it has had to use many times in the defence of cats. For instance, in 1958 a young man from Newcastle was taken to court for causing the cruel death of a kitten, but 150 years earlier such an act would have gone without public notice.

On a happier note, also in 1958 and for the second year running, Newcastle hosted the Northern Counties cat show. One of the cats on exhibition was a 'Hero' from Dublin who had saved human lives in a fire by raising the alarm.

Horses

'Home, James, and don't spare the horses!'

This saying, which has survived to our own times, sums up fairly the general attitude to horses throughout the early centuries in England, up to the late nineteenth. Certainly, they were thought of as noble, beautiful even, but it was their muscle power that was wanted. It is difficult for us nowadays to realise how complete was dependence on horses before the invention of the steam engine and later the internal combustion engine. Not only horses themselves, but all the ancillary trades associated with them took up much of old commerce, as figures from Newcastle illustrate.

In 1778 Newcastle though prosperous had a population of no more than about 30,000. Nevertheless, the commercial *Whitehead's Newcastle Directory* for that year listed within the town limits ten farriers who were also blacksmiths, five curriers, fifteen hackney horse keepers and nine hackney chaises (a chaise was a coach and horse to be hired together), as well as nine saddlers, two whip-makers and fifty-one carriers (carriers were transporters of goods overland using draught horses). Of course, people with money kept their own coaches and horses and riding horses.

A word of caution must be entered about trade directory figures. Like the Yellow Pages of today, they listed only those firms that paid to be included: the real number of practitioners in any trade could have been much higher than the directories suggest. For the same reason, it could certainly not have been lower.

By 1824, stagecoach services had added greatly to the number of horses being employed. Newcastle had twenty-four such services, the main destinations being Durham, Carlisle, Edinburgh, Leeds and London. The stagecoaches were the first form of long-distance travel available to ordinary people rather than just the wealthy. It will be recalled that stagecoach horses were required to pull heavily-laden coaches for one 'stage' of a long journey. For instance, in the journey from Newcastle to London, the first stage might be Newcastle-Darlington, the second Darlington-York etc. At the end of their stage, horses were supposed to rest as they had been running at high speed all the way. But if a stagecoach coming the other way needed horses for its own final stage, the first horses were sometimes harnessed up again and made to run the same distance with hardly any break. Visitors from the Continent thought the system cruel and the average life of a stagecoach horse was no more than two years. Worn-out stage horses were sent to knackers' yards for slaughter. Parliament passed an Act in 1824 regulating places of horse slaughter; this was almost certainly concerned with human health and hygiene rather than the

The Side, 1820: civic procession with riding horses.

Opposite above: Plough horses, Coxlodge, 1902.

Opposite below: Construction of Ouseburn culvert, 1906–07, using horsepower.

Construction of Ouseburn culvert, 1906-07, using horsepower.

suffering of the horses concerned. Despite the cruelty, stagecoaches were enormously popular in Newcastle as elsewhere. But a few decades after the height of their success, the railways began to supersede them.

At first railways only transported goods long distance, but very soon they were taking people too. By 1874 the number of stagecoach services for Newcastle and Gateshead combined was down to eleven. Large numbers of carriers were still operating – 113 for Newcastle and Gateshead – but their work was increasingly short-haul as the railway network grew. Newcastle still had plenty of farriers at this date as well as twelve horse dealers and eleven livery stables. There were many occasional horse markets and one regular one at Half Moon in the Bigg Market.

Growing consideration for the welfare of horses was shown with the installation of drinking troughs for them in all major towns. There were certainly plenty of troughs in Newcastle; some of them have been recently salvaged.

A trade directory for 1889-90 shows an *increase* in the number of horse shoers over the previous fifteen years. It has to be remembered that during those fifteen years Newcastle's

Horse-buses near the castle, 1890.

population had grown from about 135,000 to about 200,000 (the figures are for the enlarged Newcastle registration district, which included Westgate, Elswick, Jesmond, Heaton and Byker). At the same time as the railway was putting stagecoaches out of business, the swollen populations of the towns and cities required greater numbers of horses for short-distance travel and transport. In the last decades of the nineteenth century and later, Newcastle had horse-drawn trams for transport inside the city.

Horse numbers remained high all over the country until the invention of the internal combustion engine at the end of the nineteenth century. A Newcastle trade directory for 1920 listed fifteen horse-hoers, four horse dealers and fourteen saddle- and harness-makers. Crucially though, for the first time it included one automobile agent. The horse's day as the major means of transport was coming to an end.

In the 1890s many horses in Newcastle were afflicted with parasitic mange. All were treated with the remedies then available and some recovered. It is likely that they were treated for the same reason as faulty cars are mended nowadays: they cost money and their owners wanted use out of them. Nevertheless, growing compunction about the treatment and welfare of horses was shown in the annual reports of Newcastle RSPCA for the late nineteenth century.

After the Second World War, the number of horses in commercial use declined rapidly. In Newcastle the last of British Rail's horse-drawn delivery vans was taken out of service in 1950. As people no longer needed every ounce of work out of their horses they could afford to be merciful towards them. Newcastle's *Chronicle* in November 1952 carried a story about 'Old Bob', a retired carthorse destined to be slaughtered unless the Northern Counties Horse Protection Society could raise £30 for him, this being the sum the slaughterman had offered. The *Chronicle*

Farming family with two work-horses, *c.* 1910. Note the animals' overgrown hooves.

Quayside, *c.* 1908: construction work using horsepower.

The Side, 1840: heavy-goods wagon and tired carthorse.

appealed to its readers who 'responded magnificently' and 'Old Bob' retired to the country for the rest of his life. One elderly woman sent the money she had saved to buy a new coat. One cannot imagine such a thing happening a hundred years earlier.

The falling demand for draught horses after the Second World War coincided with the government's attempt to get people to eat horsemeat, supplies of beef being limited. This led to the gruesome practice of 'meat' horses being bled before slaughter in order to lighten the colour of the flesh. When this became known, in part through the *Chronicle*'s investigative journalism, there was a public outcry. Schoolchildren in particular were horrified. This tells us how greatly attitudes had changed in less than a century. The practice became outlawed and in a short time the demand for horsemeat dwindled to almost nothing.

Returning to the mid-nineteenth century, how were all those horses cared for? We can assume that tradesmen's own horses were treated fairly well on the whole because they were valuable: a carter's or a hackney coachman's livelihood depended on the health and strength of his horses. But dray horses and stagecoach horses were often ill-used and so were some people's riding horses. Newcastle RSPCA's first annual report has already been mentioned. It praised Newcastle as having a comparatively good reputation over treatment of animals and went on to say that most instances of cruelty found here were not deliberate but the result of asking too much of horses:

> Nearly all the offences hereabout consist in overloading and beating horses. The steep gradients leading from the lower to the upper parts of the town, and the roads in the suburbs contiguous to. . . collieries are the scenes of most of the cruelty which is practised in Newcastle.

The Side, 1860: carthorses and coach horses and a steam train on the bridge.

Quayside, 1900: brewers' dray horses.

Another example of 'thoughtless' cruelty was the use of the bearing-rein on riding horses, a fault chiefly committed by the upper and middle classes. The rein forced a horse's head up and certainly made it look gallant, but the unnatural position continued for long periods of time led to much unexplained illness in horses and prevented them using their full strength. We see here that the RSPCA was not afraid to criticise the upper classes; it has been suggested, wrongly in my opinion, that nineteenth-century animal-welfare measures were a covert device used by the upper classes to control the lower ones. This argument will be examined more closely later.

One Newcastle RSPCA member spoke of another 'thoughtless' cruelty. He said he had seen draught horses in Dean Street 'frightfully loaded... invariably the lads who drove these poor animals inflicted terrible punishment, and endeavoured to get the horses to perform what really they should never be asked to do.' The question arises though: on whose orders were the boys whipping the horses? This occurred to many seeking to improve animal welfare in the nineteenth century. In some of the relevant debates in Parliament and council chambers up and down the country, including Newcastle, the point was made that a horse's handler was often stressed and overworked too. One Newcastle councillor asked the other members to imagine a carter with an impossible number of orders to fulfil, who was himself perhaps not quite well and whose horse was being uncooperative. How many people in such a circumstance would act with nothing but tenderness towards the horse? So long as everyone relied on horses for every form of transport it was, I think, inevitable that cruelty would occur. Not all people were patient and principled but all wanted their journeys quick and their goods

Quayside with horse and cart in 1854, just before an extensive fire.

Quayside with pony and cart in 1854, after the fire.

Ice-cream cart and pony, *c.* 1920.

Newburn Carnival, decorated carthorse, *c.* 1910.

on time, especially those who gave orders to servants. As we have seen, it was when people could *afford* to be merciful to horses that they became so; they could afford to because there were now engines and motors to do the work. The ill-treatment of horses is referred to in the chapter dealing with the animal-cruelty debates which continued throughout the nineteenth century.

England, of course, was not the only horse-dependent nation at that time. One English traveller reported that, in parts of Europe, this country was regarded as 'hell for horses'. Another who had visited Turkey said the Turks treated their horses kindly, especially the foals, with the result that their horses were 'fond and obedient'. It has to be admitted that the English in the nineteenth century and probably earlier were not good horse-masters. Newcastle people were certainly no worse than others; according to the RSPCA they were better.

On a lighter if stranger note, a *Chronicle* report from back in 1731 described a travelling exhibition in Newcastle that featured a six-legged horse. To end with, here is a nursery rhyme that was still being sung when the writer was a child; it illustrates the cold-hearted view of horses that prevailed for many centuries until the Victorian welfare measures began to take effect:

John Cook had a little grey mare, hee, haw, hum,
Her back stood up and her bones were bare, hee, haw, hum.
John Cook went riding up Shooter's bank, hee, haw, hum,
And there his mare did kick and prank, hee, haw, hum.
John Cook went riding up Shooter's hill, hee, haw, hum,
His mare fell down and she made her will, hee, haw, hum.

Pit Ponies

Another member of the horse family figures largely in Newcastle's history: the pit pony. Coal has been mined in and around Newcastle for about 800 years and a charter of Henry III in 1239 granted the town the right to mine and sell coal anywhere subject to port custom duties; from that time on, coal was a major economic mover in Newcastle's development. This development relied not so much on the town's own mines as on its transporting coal from outlying ones. It was estimated in 1800 that 6,530 pitmen were employed in Newcastle, though not all of them would be face-workers. The number of pits within the town limits depended, of course, on where those limits were drawn. For instance, the collieries at Gosforth and Byker in the mid-eighteenth century were not inside Newcastle, nor were the slightly later ones at Benwell, Wideopen, Longbenton, Walker and Fawdon. But Newcastle dealt with their output and they were often referred to loosely as being in Newcastle. Newcastle also handled the coal from collieries further afield, such as Ashington, Wallsend, Howden, Willington and Percy Main. One colliery inside Newcastle itself and mentioned in a report of 1844 was the St Lawrence pit. A 1922 report by HM Inspectors of Mines listed five working collieries in Newcastle itself: Hazelrigg, Benwell 'Charlotte', Elswick North, Elswick South and Scotswood Drift.

As to the lives of the miners and, our concern here, the working ponies, an 1860 description of a descent into the coal pit is illuminating:

> Then, in a minute or two, you distinguish the men at the shaft bottom, and the sluggish oil lamp, and the little lads coming up with their train of coal wagons; then the horses or ponies, being unfastened from one load and conveyed inward to draw another. Now you can see the remarkable smoothness of the horses' coats, and the sleekness of the ponies' appearance. The horses get fat, the men lean; the ponies well-conditioned and the lads ill-conditioned. The horses and ponies are conveyed down the pit in large nets; of course, they seldom get up again, but live night and day down in their underground stalls…

Indeed, William Cobbett of *Rural Rides* fame wrote about mines in another work:

> Here is the most surprising thing in the whole world; thousands of men and thousands of horses continually living under ground: children born there, and who sometimes never see the surface at all, though they live to a considerable age!!

Pit pony in bare stall. Other ponies had straw to lie on.

However, that description cannot have applied to Newcastle or its surrounding area – in our pits no women were ever employed underground so no babies could have been born there. What is more, some of our collieries got the ponies up to the surface for a few weeks every year; it seems more would have done so had it not been for the huge difficulty of getting them up and down the mineshaft. Some Durham pits used to race the ponies they 'brought up' during August and this was a popular sport. I could not discover whether this happened in Newcastle.

In her book, *My Pit Pony*, Joan Gale spelled out the work the animals did. The mine she described was at Bedlington in the second half of the twentieth century. By then conditions were very much improved for the ponies and had been since the Coal Mines Act of 1911. It is significant that this legislation covered the animals as well as the human workers in the mines:

It was black gloom down in the pit, with dingy lights strung along the low roof and thick grey coal dust underfoot. [A pony's] job was to pull two heavy coal tubs along a narrow railway line, with a pitman walking behind the trucks. Each tub held half a ton of coal. The pit ponies wore bridles with a thick leather piece in front to protect their heads from falling stone and other hazards. The tubs were attached by a bolt (rather like the fitting used for hitching a trailer to a motor vehicle) to a pair of U-shaped shafts known as 'limmers'. These short shafts passed through the tugs of a small sturdy pad on the pony's back, and were connected to the collar by chains. Both the pit collar and the pad were lined with coarse woolen material, in a black and white check pattern. Sometimes the pitman would steal a ride by sitting on the limmers, but this was frowned on as dangerous in the narrow confines of the pit seams.

After the ponies had done their shift... they were taken to the underground stables, each stall not much larger than a child's cot, with a sprinkling of sawdust for bedding. Every day after work they were given a shower from an overhead hose-pipe, to clean off the coal-dust and sweat, although they were clipped quite bare, with manes and tails cut short because of the warm atmosphere in the pit, and to avoid getting caught in any machinery...

Pit ponies' *lives* rather than their work were well described by F. Zwerg writing in 1948:

The ponies are brought into pits at the age of four, and stay there their whole lives up to eighteen or twenty. It takes a pony about two years to get used to the underground conditions and to develop its full pit-sense...

Many ponies have a better pit-sense than men, and they refuse to go to unsafe places. In fact... ponies [have] saved men from being killed.

They work a full shift [throughout most of the nineteenth century this was twelve hours!], then they are fed and cleaned in the stables underground... Some stables are very good and clean and well-lit. Others have a stone floor covered with dirt. A pony kept clean, often washed, works better... [The] ponies also have their limit. If they are used to drive two tubs, and you tried to impose on them an extra burden, they would refuse to move. They also work better for some men for whom they have an affection than for others.

'Are the ponies happy in the pits?' I asked the old horse-keeper.

'Why not?' he replied. 'If you feed them, clean them and treat them properly, they are happy. They are used to the pits and don't mind working in them... After a week's holiday the older ones would go willingly by themselves to the winding-cage, and you don't need to force them to go down.'

Pit ponies' food was the subject of competing theories in the nineteenth century. Charles Hunting, veterinary surgeon to Trimdon Grange Colliery in Co. Durham, produced a treatise on the subject which was first read to the Newcastle Farmers' Club in 1860. It explained a horse's digestive system in detail and condemned the old and largely discontinued practice of not feeding the ponies at all during their twelve- to fourteen-hour shifts, instead giving them a large meal at the end. Mr Hunting maintained that this resulted in severe digestive problems, sometimes ending in death. Happily, things had changed by the time he gave his paper. One passage said:

Since 1850 at every station, flat and siding where animals stop, if only for two minutes, there is hay, and at all principal places water. As a result, at South Hetton and Murton collieries, out of 225 animals, we have had only 19 cases of digestive disorder in seven years.

From this, we see that mine owners in the North East were ready to correct mistakes when these were pointed out.

Worn-out pit ponies sometimes met a cruel end. In 1875, a scandal was uncovered by the Newcastle RSPCA: aged pit ponies were being bought by townsmen and used to cart coal from the collieries. Such heavy carting work was too hard for old animals, one of which had been seen to be 'stone-blind'. One member of the society's board, who was a pit owner himself, said he would ensure none of his own old pit ponies were sold into such servitude and he undertook to inform fellow pit owners of the practise. In 1881 Mr Ralph Carr-Ellison, JP, announced that he had discovered the source of retired pit ponies being worked to death by townspeople. Some colliery owners in Gateshead, Felling and Hebburn were the culprits; they regularly took their ponies for sale at the Stones Fair in Newcastle or other horse marts. All who heard this account vowed to do whatever they could to end the misuse. It seems they were successful – no later council minutes mentioned any such buying and selling of old pit ponies.

By the mid-twentieth century and probably earlier, some were being bought and sold for light work by considerate owners. One of these owners was Joan Gale, whose description of a Bedlington mine has already been quoted. The retired pit pony that she bought, which she christened the Earl of Bedlington, was at first upset by life above ground. He was unused to the cold air and the blowing of the wind; birdsong made him jump. Neither was he happy being handled by a woman. All this suggests that his life underground had not been actively unhappy. Eventually he became used to his new life as a trap pony pulling a light carriage. Her book, of course, is written from her point of view, not the pony's. One cannot help wondering what is the difference, for a pony, between pulling a light carriage and pulling a light cartful of coal. Perhaps the offence of the 'cruel' buyers was simply one of overloading their carts. As to Miss Gale, one hopes her 'light carriage' was never crammed with an entire family, heavy members included!

Cattle and Other Livestock

Until the late nineteenth century, cattle, sheep, pigs and other animals were driven – i.e. made to walk or trot – from the farms on which they were bred to a market. There they were bought by wholesalers, by drovers employed to conduct them across country, by slaughterers or by local butchers who did their own slaughtering. Sometimes farmers bought animals to improve their own stock. As a result, country roads and the streets of all towns were frequently thronged with animals going to and from market and bringing other traffic to a halt. This was usual throughout the whole country and only changed, so far as long distances were concerned, with the spread of the railways in the mid- and late nineteenth century. But right into the twentieth century, it was common to see herds of animals being moved through towns. Legislation for the welfare of cattle began in 1823 with an Act forbidding cruel and improper use; two years later the scope of the Act was enlarged. (These Acts were a sign that the concept of 'reform' in British society went far beyond political and commercial matters. Slowly, the whole concept of *laissez-faire* which had imbued the previous century was being questioned and found wanting.)

As well as providing meat, slaughtered animals were the source of skins, bones and fat – all of which formed the bases of ancillary trades. In 1827, according to *Parson & White's Trade Directory for Newcastle*, in one district alone, Ouseburn, there was a tannery, a soap manufactory and a greaseworks. Writing of this area in Bygone Lower Ouseburn, Alan Morgan says: 'farmers, stables, slaughterhouses, bone and glue works, butchers, sawmills and tanneries existed more or less side by side…' With regard to soap manufacture, *Parson & White's* lists soap as one of Newcastle's exports. Most butchers did their own slaughtering, although later in the century those who were members of the Butchers' Co. may have used the organisation's slaughterhouse at Blackfriars.

In 1850 a large cattle market was built on what is now the site of the Centre for Life. It was enlarged in 1873 to become the biggest in the North, exceeding even Glasgow's in size. It is clear that Newcastle Council, whose enterprise this was, took animal welfare into account as it stipulated that the floor be '…laid with cement concrete, checked [i.e. roughened] on the surface so that cattle may keep their foothold.' Pigs were to be penned under cover in view of their lack of fur. From 1867 to 1874 the number of cattle brought to market annually doubled to 79,433.

Concern for animal welfare was shown in the regulation that sheep must not be brought to market shorn in cold wet weather. (Regulations were in the nature of bye-laws suggested by the government; local authorities could chose to adopt them or not and Newcastle had adopted this

From top right: Sheep being driven through The Close, 1898; two entrants in the fat cattle class, Newcastle Agricultural Show, *c.* 1910; the winner of the Newcastle Fat Cattle Show, 1930/1.

Sheep being driven under the Tyne Bridge to market, 1950s.

Opposite above: Ruins of Blackfriars, site of an old slaughterhouse.

Opposite below: Cattle market, *c.* 1920. On this site is the present Centre for Life.

Sheep grazing on Town Moor.

one.) But there was opposition to some of the measures: Mr Ralph Ellison wrote to Newcastle's recently founded RSPCA protesting that sheep did not mind being cold or wet. They were, he pronounced, 'happy animals very little oppressed by cruelty'! Nevertheless, despite disagreeing with the regulation, he increased his annual subscription to the society to £5.

British home-grown meat was of very fine quality and, despite being plentiful, expensive. To meet the need for cheap meat that poor people could afford, foreign cattle were imported as soon as it became practicable to do so. The Tyne needed to be dredged to allow the passage of ships into the town centre: when this had been done, cattle importing started in earnest. In the early years, most imports were from Scandinavia and the trade throve to such an extent that many Danish and Swedish merchants set up in business here. It is surprising to discover that for some decades of the nineteenth century Newcastle carried on a barter trade with Iceland, i.e. one in which no money was exchanged. The town (later city) exported manufactured goods to Iceland and, on the return journey, imported Icelandic sheep. Imported animals had a cruel welcome. Newcastle RSPCA's 1876 annual report said:

> From the first moment the cattle landed from the steamers they were surrounded by children of between three and fourteen, with sticks and all sorts of things, with which they struck the animals on their eyes, head, nose, or anywhere they could. And they seemed to have a delight in doing it. It was not very much to the credit of the cattle salesmen. . . that they employed these children. To employ men they would have to pay them properly.

The children were paid a few pennies each for their unofficial drover work – money which they welcomed. It was many decades before children in towns stopped tormenting cattle in this way.

Calves with young cowherd, Ouseburn, 1919.

Indeed, only a few days ago I was reading the life story of one well-known person in which he said that one of the features of his happy early childhood in York was chasing and beating calves on their way to market.

A cattle sanatorium was built in 1876-7 on the west bank of the Ouseburn just north of its junction with the Tyne. It was a quarantine holding centre for imported cattle and for home-grown ones which had arrived in Newcastle and were showing signs of ill health. It had a capacity of 635 cattle and 3,000 sheep at a time. Animals were held for twelve hours before being inspected by a veterinary surgeon. Those free of disease were driven to the market; infected animals were slaughtered on the spot. The cattle sanatorium was rarely full but demands were growing for an additional one, quite separate, to accommodate animals from countries where bovine diseases were endemic. Separation was needed to prevent infection of other animals.

Different demands were also being made on the city fathers concerning the whole business of the marketing and slaughtering of animals. People were complaining about the huge volume of animal traffic trekking to and fro through the city streets and there was the suspicion that Newcastle's numerous private slaughterhouses were a health hazard. One councillor said that more animal blood was shed in one week than was seen in a major battle. Moreover, that blood was being washed down public drains and into the river. And demand for meat was growing, not diminishing, as the population grew. Many people suggested that the whole business would be better managed beyond residential areas. (One can see this as the beginning of the 'out of sight, out of mind' attitude to animal slaughter which still prevails today.)

In 1884-5, the cattle import trade together with other facilities were moved down-river to St Lawrence, which at that time was sparsely populated, and the extra sanatorium built there. Ironically, by the 1890s the import of cattle was dwindling countrywide. There were a number

Above: Disused cattle sanatorium at Ouseburn, 1899.

Left: Cattle grazing on Town Moor.

of reasons for this: (1) building and staffing the additional sanatoria was expensive, (2) many foreign cattle, especially those from Spain and the Americas, were now as good as home-grown animals and therefore their meat was no cheaper, (3) the invention of refrigeration meant that carcasses could be shipped between countries instead of live animals.

Cattle diseases were as prevalent then as they are now. Throughout the nineteenth century and later, herds in the North East were regularly attacked by foot-and-mouth disease and bovine tuberculosis, whilst swine fever laid waste to pigs. In 1865 the dreaded rinderpest exacted its toll on the cattle of the North East, a toll added to by the policy of compulsory slaughter to contain the infection. A contemporary record says: '. . . all throughout Newcastle, in a few weeks, there was scarcely a byre but had been laid waste, not so much from the disease as the indiscriminate use of the axe by order of the inspectors.' As I write, exactly the same policy is being enacted in the South of England over cases of foot-and-mouth.

Pigs

Until factory-farming methods were introduced in the second half of the twentieth century, pigs reared for food had a fairly comfortable life, although certainly not their natural one of foraging in the woodlands for nuts, roots and fungi. They were sheltered, well fed as to quantity and variety and, except for the boars, given the run of the farmyard.

Pork and bacon were (and are) as popular in Newcastle as elsewhere and pigs were often referred to in cattle-market reports. They do not seem to have raised many welfare concerns, apart from the stipulation already mentioned that they should have sheltered accommodation in the cattle market. In 1923, a cattle-market inspector noted that in the weeks leading up to Christmas pigs were suffering and sometimes dying in the stock markets because of overcrowding; he urged the building of extra accommodation for them. We shall see that the humane methods of slaughter introduced in Newcastle in the 1920s did not at first apply to pigs. But over time the compassionate argument prevailed.

During the Second World War, various pig clubs were formed in and around the city to augment the food supply. Residents of an area clubbed together to buy pigs which they then kept on whichever bits of land, or even of garden space, they had spare. The pigs were fed on kitchen food waste; a portion of the resulting pork and bacon went to the Ministry of Food, the rest was for the pig-club members themselves. From my own childhood (not in Newcastle), I remember my mother and others in the street having 'pig bins' where food waste was saved. Each evening the 'pig man' came to empty the bins into a large container, drawn by a horse, which was then taken to where the pigs were. But feeding pigs had its problems during the war because people were urged not to waste food. Of course the pigs could not be fed on the precious grain, potatoes etc. which were needed for the human population. The Heaton Pig Club was particularly successful and kept its herd for many years.

In the 'austerity' years immediately after the war, pigs were, therefore, in short supply. In 1947 the country was set the target of producing 1 million extra pigs; whether this was ever achieved we do not know. At the time, the biggest pig enterprise in the Northern counties was the 'Canny' herd of pedigree Large Whites owned by Mr William Walker, who kept them at South Gosforth. In the meantime, the country's bacon needs were being met by imports from Canada.

In 1970 Newcastle University's department of agriculture claimed to have bred the 'perfect pig'. It was a hybrid of a Belgian Piétrain boar and an English Large White sow. The university announced that the meat from the resulting offspring was being tested at the time of writing on the open market and certainly the chops were selling well.

The following year saw the introduction of one of the unquestionably cruel 'factory-farming' methods being implemented by the government, no doubt as part of the effort to get numbers of animals up. The metal farrowing stall for sows, which had been invented in Sweden, prevented a sow from moving before, during and after the birth process. Mr Ted Garrett, MP for Wallsend, described it as a 'fiendish contraption'. Alas, it was soon adopted across the whole country and remained the standard fate for farrowing sows before being finally banned at the end of the twentieth century.

Through the decades, indeed through the centuries, the *Newcastle Chronicle* carried regular reports of pigs escaping on their way to the slaughterhouse and running through the town: sooner or later all were recaptured.

Heaton pig farm during the Second World War.

Heaton pig farm during the Second World War.

Byker City Farm

In 1976 the site of an old lead-paint works at lower Ouseburn Valley was decontaminated and cleared in order to establish Byker City Farm as part of the regeneration of the region. In 1981 the last of several additional fields was added and for some years the farm attracted great numbers of visitors, both local and from farther afield. Sadly, in 2002 contamination was discovered at the site once again and the farm closed for the foreseeable future. Stepney Bank Stables, who run various riding schools, still use the land to graze their horses.

Cow in summer field, Byker Farm.

Sheep and ponies at Byker Farm.

Above: Jersey cow, Byker Farm.

Left: Goats under Metro Bridge, Byker Farm.

Slaughter

This is a sad and grim subject but no account of animals reared for food can avoid it. Newcastle introduced the 'humane killer' in the 1920s, originally for large animals only but later for sheep and pigs too. Before that date, large animals in Newcastle were killed with a rope and hammer, as reported below. Other towns used other methods. I imagine the rope and hammer were a means of stunning the animals before they had their throats cut. Sheep and pigs simply had their throats cut without pre-stunning. Calves intended for veal were bled to death slowly over several hours: this practice was outlawed at the end of the nineteenth century. Nowadays we can take comfort in the knowledge that animals reared for meat in this country (excepting chickens) have reasonably comfortable lives and quick, painless deaths.

Here is a first-hand account of the driving and slaughtering of cattle in the early decades of the twentieth century, recollected in 1961 by an ex-slaughterman:

> It is difficult to imagine Shields Road as a country lane, but there were faint resemblances now and then even in the two decades before the last war [the Second World War]. Even then sheep and cattle were driven along the road to the slaughterhouse up the hill.
>
> Sometimes the animals would break away from their procession to run about the back lanes between the houses.
>
> The children loved this to happen and with screams and yells would join the drovers in trying to get the animals back to the road. For a time there would be confusion and noise, and for a time Byker could imagine itself back in its rural past.

City abattoir, 1967.

City abattoir, 1967.

Mr David Walker, nearly seventy, recalls working in the 'killing house' where he used to slaughter cattle with a rope and hammer. Interestingly, he mentions the introduction of the humane killer:

> It were a nasty business... but then one day there came a chap with a new idea. He had a gun and told me I'd got to use that to kill the beast. [This would be an early captive bolt pistol.] But we had to get his head still first and this meant getting hold of the horns. Man, I divna like that at all. Those beasts were angry and those great horns were dangerous. I'm telling you they could kill a man, so Ah left them to their humane killer. Mind you, Ah expect it were better for the beast. The hammer and rope way was no good, but Ah left them and went into the shipyards.

Butchers
In 1778, with a population of about 30,000, Newcastle had fifty-five butchers listed in *Whitehead's Trade Directory*. By 1839 this figure had increased to 151, excluding a number working in Gateshead.

Newcastle's population had more than doubled in the intervening sixty years, which probably explains the huge increase in the number of butchers. In 1839, fourteen tallow chandlers were also listed – these were manufacturers of candles from beef fat. The 1874-5 directory had a massive total of 254 butchers, though this figure possibly included Gateshead. No wonder councillors complained of the nuisance and bloodshed. Listed separately from butchers were thirty-one game and poultry dealers, seven hide-and-skin merchants and fourteen leather-and-hide merchants, though it is difficult to see what could have been the difference between 'hide-and-skin' and 'leather-and-hide'. There was also a separate entry for eighteen tripe preparers. Tripe in those days was a cheap and nutritious meal for those who could not afford red meat – certainly not the culinary specialty it is now. By 1876-7 the number of tripe preparers had risen to twenty-one; tallow chandlers had fallen to eight and butchers fallen slightly to 240. In 1885 there were only 202 butchers – possibly the result of amalgamation between small firms – but fifty-six game and poultry dealers. Interesting entries in the 1874-5 directory included a few guano merchants!

Outdoor poultry market, *c.* 1890.

Leathards grocers selling bacon.

Left: Butcher's shop, Grainger Market.

Below: Butcher's shop, Grainger Market.

Dairy Cows

As there was no fast transport to bring milk into towns until the advent of railways and no way to keep it fresh until the invention of refrigeration, milch cows in early centuries lived in town dairies and were milked twice a day. The milk was sold immediately or saved to make butter and cheese. All of this was the work of dairymen and women. In Newcastle they bought their cows at the Cow Market in Newgate Street, possibly where The Gate complex now stands. Farmers or drovers brought the cows into town, sometimes with calves at their heels.

In the eighteenth and early nineteenth centuries in Newcastle, milk was sold at the Milk Market in Sandgate. An 1820 illustration of the Milk Market shows no cows, but they must have been in the locality since there was no way then of keeping milk fresh once it had been drawn. Perhaps dairymen kept their animals in yards behind the buildings or in cellars underneath them. At that date also perhaps all dairymen plied their trade at the same place in the old medieval way. By 1865 though, Newcastle had at least thirty-five dairies located in all parts of the town and none of them listed their address as 'Milk Market'.

Dairymen and women sold milk, cheese and butter from shops attached to their dairies; they also sold door to door, the milk being carried in a metal churn transported by a pony and cart. Measuring pots with long handles for dipping into the churn would measure a quart, a pint, a half-pint, and a quarter-pint, called a gill. Well into the twentieth century this was the usual way to buy milk in country areas; a hundred years earlier townspeople bought it that way too. In *Whitehead's Newcastle Trade Directory* for 1778, twenty-one cheesemongers were listed and some of these would certainly have been dairymen and women as well. *Christie's Directory* for 1874-5 gave seventy-two dairymen, but two years later only forty-six were listed. One possible explanation for this decline is that the earlier figure included Gateshead and the later one did not.

The Cow Market in Newgate Street was the scene of the unkind practice of 'overstocking'. This meant bringing cows to market unmilked, sometimes with their teats sealed up with grains of rice so that the udder swelled enormously. Dairymen, always on the lookout for the most productive animals, knowingly or unknowingly bought these bloated cows. Some Newcastle councillors in the 1880s protested strongly against the practice, even though the market's veterinary surgeon had said that it was not cruel. One councillor advised his colleagues to ask their wives (if they were married and had children) or their mothers (if they were not) whether overstocking was cruel. When the subject next came up in council, it was found that the ladies had been unanimous in condemning it as cruel.

Milk Market, 1820.

Cow with newborn calf. Calves were often brought to the Cow Market with their mothers. (courtesy of Mary Evans Picture Library)

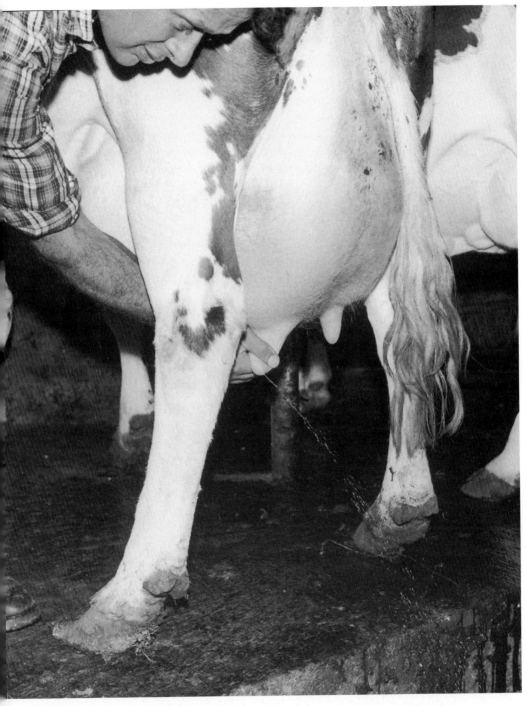

Swollen udder. Cows were 'overstocked' (though this one was not) to achieve this result.

An Act of Parliament was passed in 1883 extending the existing regulations on cowsheds, dairies and milk shops. It is possible that part of the Act covered the cows' own wellbeing, but we can be sure that its main purpose was to safeguard human health. If we contrast this with the Newcastle councillors' condemnation of overstocking, we can see that at least in some respects Newcastle was ahead of other places in considering animal welfare.

Overstocking was not the only evil seen in the Cow Market. Alderman Richard Cail wrote to the council to protest that:

> [T]he cows were driven there [Newgate Street] and stood in fives and sixes up to tens, and every time a cart passed the animals were scattered helter-skelter in all directions. They... were overstocked to such an extent that the slightest movement must cause the animals a large amount of pain... He had seen cows go to the market straight from byres on the very morning they had calved... the state the poor beasts were in... they chased one another back and forward, and ran against conveyances and people.

It was proposed to move the Cow Market to somewhere quieter with less traffic, perhaps the Haymarket.

The invention of refrigeration changed all this, not at a stroke but relentlessly over the decades. Once milk became not immediately perishable, it could be collected from milking parlours on the farms, refrigerated and delivered to retailers in the towns. Eventually of course every home had a refrigerator. This is not the only example of technological advances easing the suffering of animals or, even more so, of humans.

Dairy cows on Leazes Moor, 1902.

of the Walker Training Farm, learning the art of milking, which
les part of their tuition.

Walker Training Farm, 1929: imitation udders.

Newcastle Races, Brough Park, Pigeon Racing

The first written reference to Newcastle Races occurs in the corporation's accounts for 1632 whilst Charles I was on the throne. Later, during Oliver Cromwell's protectorate, all horse racing was suppressed – in theory at least. It was reinstated with the restoration of the monarchy in 1660. At this date, Newcastle Races were held on Killingworth Moor. By 1721 races were taking place daily, so great was the taste for them, and the preferred venue was Town Moor. An Act of 1740 suppressed 'petty races... held annually at almost every village in the country', thus showing the taste for racing was countrywide. One paragraph of this Act decreed that no race should be held with plate or stake less than £50. This could suggest an attempt to stop poor people taking part in the sport, or alternatively to stop people of all classes frittering away their working days at the racecourse. (Modern measures applied to other 'vices' can also be read either way, for instance, increasing the price of alcohol.) The effect of the 1740 Act was to cut down Newcastle's racing days to three per week: the Innkeepers' Plate on Tuesdays, the Freemans' Plate on Wednesdays and the Gold Cup on Thursdays. But these restrictions did not suit the popular mood and were therefore eroded bit by bit, until by the mid-1750s Newcastle had races on five days a week, some of them sweepstakes. In 1785 a race was held between two mules, each ridden by its owner. The competing riders were Sir H.G. Liddell and Mr Richard Bell; Mr Bell won.

Gambling was the national craze of the late seventeenth and eighteenth centuries and bets were placed on all manner of contests including blood sports. A 1721 advertisement for Newcastle Races also announced: 'for the gentlemen's diversion, Cock-fighting every forenoon at Mr Hill's pit.' Mr Hill was the owner or licensee of the Black Bull and Crown public house. He was also clerk to the course at Newcastle Races, a fact which conveys well the *laissez-faire* tenor of the eighteenth century. From 1712, cockfighting had in fact been advertised at other venues such as the Turk's Head in the Bigg Market, owned by Mr William Parker. Another notice dated 1720 announced: 'A Free Plate, value 2 guineas, by hounds, a Trail Scent of a live fox, six miles; no gentleman allowed to shout or cap his dog, under the penalty of losing the Plate.' This plate seems to have been a single event that was not repeated.

Like other races, the Northumberland Plate – a straightforward race for horses – was held on Town Moor from the early nineteenth century; in 1833 the winner was recorded as Tomboy. By 1881 the venue of this famous race had changed from Town Moor to High Gosforth Park, which had brand-new flat and chase courses, plus stabling for 100 horses. Gosforth Park had been developed by speculators who wanted to make the sport more professional and, no doubt, more lucrative. But the move caused an outcry in the town as race days on Town

Grandstand, Town Moor, 1840.

Newcastle Races, 1912.

Gosforth Park, Grandstand, 1930.

Plate Day, Gosforth Park, 1952.

Racing greyhounds, Brough Park.

Group of greyhounds. (courtesy of Mary Evans Picture Library)

Moor were a much-loved feature of Newcastle life. Marks of the old course can be seen on the moor to this day. So the transfer went ahead in the teeth of protest, but in time people got used to travelling to Gosforth Park if they wanted to follow racing. The racecourse became, and remains, one of the most important in the country, with its own traditions. One of these is Beeswing Ladies' Day, named after a famous mare who never won the Northumberland Plate, although she won forty-six of her fifty-one races.

Brough Park

Official greyhound racing began in Newcastle in 1928 at Brough Park, where it continues to this day. Unofficial dog racing has a long history and probably originated as an offshoot of hare coursing.

The course at Brough Park has been used for other kinds of races too, notably the Donkey Derby which was popular from the 1930s to the 1980s. This annual event has sometimes attracted 10,000 spectators. The Donkey Derby featured more than donkeys racing each other: there was also pony trotting and displays of boxing, sprinting and gymnastics. One race pitted a pony against a man from a standing start. Professional jockeys would ride donkeys for charity at Brough Park and in 1953 (coronation year) two jockeys fell! One of them had to push his steed for ten yards and the winner coaxed his mount over the finishing line with a carrot! Another jockey crossed the line facing backwards. But the most unusual event must be one of the races in 1954, pitting bikes against cheetahs. We are not told where the cheetahs came from.

Pigeon fanciers putting a ring on to their bird.

Pigeon crees on Skinnerburn Road.

Pigeon Racing

The Newcastle upon Tyne Homing Society was formed in 1892. Unlike most pigeon-racing clubs in the country, its membership was not exclusively working class. Local businessmen, doctors, innkeepers and colliery officials were among the members. Indeed, the sport came to appeal more and more to the middle classes over the years. The *LMS Magazine* noted in 1929 that:

> At the time of its inception, some 40 years ago, pigeon racing was considered to be essentially a working man's hobby, but this is no longer the case, and many of the newspapers in their account of the Bournemouth race, stated that the owners of the birds taking part in the flight comprised members of all ranks of society.

As to our own region, the winner of the first 'Up North Combine' race in 1905 was a baker and confectioner with his own shop and bakery in Jarrow. But, at the time of its beginnings, pigeon racing was a working-class sport. One researcher, Alan Metcalfe, found definite evidence of homing clubs in Northumberland mining villages in 1877 and circumstantial evidence of much earlier dates for the sport. In those early years it was everywhere a local sport with short-distance races; only in the 1890s (when the Newcastle club began) did long-distance racing become popular. The time lag is surprising since the idea of racing pigeons for sport was probably a result of the birds' official use by governments and commercial concerns to take messages to and from Europe. Personally I suspect an additional origin for the hobby: namely the keeping of pigeons for shooting.

By 1905 the volume of pigeon-fancy traffic on the railways from the mining districts of Northumberland was so heavy the North Eastern Railway Co. began to run pigeon specials.

Nationally, pigeon keeping was considered a nuisance in the nineteenth century; people complained that building lofts for the birds weakened timber structures and that their droppings caused wood to rot. In Bolton, Lancashire, in the 1850s the inspector of nuisances tried to get it banned. However, during the First World War (1914-18), pigeons showed their worth as message carriers for the military; this restored them, and the pigeon fancy itself, to respectability.

During the Second World War the sale of foodstuff for pigeons was discontinued and this led to large numbers of the birds being slaughtered. Some of these were sold to butchers for 9d or 1s each and then resold to the public for 1s or 1s 3d. The government asked owners to keep no more than ten pairs each. At the same time, pigeon fanciers in the North East donated young birds to the National Pigeon Service for military use. Some pigeons won the Dickin Medal (the animals' VC) for war service.

Racing pigeons were never neglected or ill-treated, except by accident. Owners of lofts were and are proud of their birds and cared for them well. If you walk westward along the north bank of the Tyne from Newcastle city centre you will pass many pigeon lofts. On fine days all the birds of one loft seem to 'go for a fly' just like people going for a walk. They stay more or less together; they circle and swoop, head off in one direction, swerve off in another, soar upward, turn and plunge again, apparently with no purpose but the sheer pleasure of flight. After ten or twenty minutes they alight in twos and threes, cooing, on the roof of their loft. I cannot believe discontented birds would seem so happy.

There was one practice, which may or may not be discontinued now and could be described as unkind, even though not downright cruel: sometimes a newly-mated bird would be deliberately separated from its mate, which would be kept grounded, just before being entered for a race. The separation made the racing bird so anxious to return that it would strive to be back, flying with utmost effort over the whole distance and therefore having a better chance of winning. It can be argued that such situations must often occur in the wild; the reply is that in the wild the mate would be free to fly too.

Blood Sports

I have used the term 'blood sports' rather than 'field sports' because some of the practices described took place in towns or suburbs rather than the open country. The Northumberland and Durham aristocracy hunted, shot and fished the same as others of their class everywhere and so did many of the clergy. From Tudor times, the rise of the middle class meant that many merchants, manufacturers, dealers and professional men took up these pursuits as well. And there are some sports – hare coursing is one – that have always attracted spectators from all social classes. I did not intend to quote in this book from the memoirs of fox-hunting men or 'compleat anglers,' although plenty of both were published in the North East. Rather I concentrated on reports of local blood sports in the Newcastle area. Lest it seem that by describing these mainly working-class activities I have accused the working class of being more cruel than others, it should be remembered that I deliberately excluded the aristocracy's field sports as being too large a subject.

Pigeon shooting seems to have pre-dated pigeon keeping – or perhaps the keeping derived from and, in some cases, superseded the shooting. Certainly, in the second half of the nineteenth century pigeon-shooting matches were a regular part of the amusements of Newcastle people. The details are grim. The feathers of pigeons' tails and rumps were plucked out and pins and pepper pushed up their fundaments. The pain this inflicted made the birds 'surge' up in flight in a vain attempt to escape their tormentors. Thus surging directly upwards they were an excellent target for the guns.

A sport popular with boys was to tie their hands behind their backs and then chase a cockerel. The aim was to catch the bird in the boy's teeth then heave it over one shoulder. The same bird was used for however many boys took part.

Hare coursing with greyhounds was, as we have noted, indulged in by all social classes. Dogs that performed poorly had an ugly fate; some were hanged, some beaten to death. An alternative was to throw them in the river, legs tied to prevent them swimming, and watch them drown. One or two of these wretched dogs actually survived. In 1834 the *Chronicle* reported a hare being killed in Pilgrim Street, 'by hounds belonging to Mr J.G. Clark'. The hare had been 'put up' behind Kenton Lodge from where it ran to Gosforth, 'thence to the Grand Stand, afterwards across the moor into Pilgrim Street'.

Later in the century, Captain Blenkinsop-Coulson, a member of Newcastle RSPCA, gave a report to the society on hare coursing at Gosforth Park. He had observed there no human-to-animal cruelty, he said, only that of the dogs towards the hares. He recommended that RSPCA

Huntsman and hounds. (courtesy of Mary Evans Picture Library)

Unkennelling the hounds. (courtesy of Mary Evans Picture Library)

members attend hare coursing, perhaps even organise it themselves, to ensure no ill-treatment was meted out by humans. One can see the logic of this; one sees also the glaring omission of any examination of humans' desire to watch cruelty or of the question whether such desire should be pandered to. At Gosforth Park, said the captain, the hares had a sporting chance of escaping, whereas in unregulated coursing the hares were hemmed in and unable to escape. Moreover the spectators yelled to confuse each hare. I cannot help suspecting cynically that even had the RSPCA arranged 'merciful' hare courses, crueller ones would have been got up unofficially.

From the reports of the Dicky Bird Society (to be examined later) we know that boys of all classes robbed birds' nests and took eggs, stoned birds and cats, killed cats by a variety of means and generally regarded animals as a source of gory enjoyment. Throughout much of the nineteenth century, such activities were tolerated across the country, and society as a whole, as 'boyish': it seems some degree of cruelty was thought normal in boys. One of the arguments adduced early in the century for keeping the cruel sport of bull-baiting was that it made boys manly.

Rabbit catching was not a sport but a source of extra meat. Steel traps were set to catch them; they often caught other animals such as foxes. One member of Newcastle RSPCA pleaded for these traps to be banned, on the grounds that they endangered 'the fine old English sport of foxhunting'! He recommended using nets and ferrets instead. We see here another instance of the usual attitude to cruelty, or any other vice for that matter: namely, what others do may well be wicked and should be stopped, but what I do, however, is normal and should continue.

Outside observers writing about coal mines in the North East noted that pitmen here were not as cruel and barbarous as those in other parts of the country, although they liked cockfighting.

If we put together the glimpses, half-reports and occasional details of the customary treatment of animals in the nineteenth century, a picture emerges of creatures being seen not only as providers of human food, human clothes and heavy labour, but also, by means of suffering inflicted on them by men or other animals, as a natural source of human entertainment. However, alongside this we discern another picture of the growth of humanitarian feelings toward animals and eventually of legislation on their behalf. Perhaps what is called the Whig version of history is right and people do slowly become better over the centuries. Then again, perhaps the lesser amount of cruelty to animals tolerated in civilised societies today is due partly to the amount and variety of vicarious bloodshed and torture available via the media.

Newcastle RSPCA

Although affiliated with each other, all branches of the RSPCA (Royal Society for the Prevention of Cruelty to Animals) are independent organisations. The Newcastle society, which began in 1873, originally covered a huge area from Berwick in the north to Hartlepool in the south and Tynemouth in the east to Whitehaven, Cumberland, in the west. Like so many enlightened enterprises begun by the Victorians, it was a charitable endeavour and remains so to this day. Interested individuals contributed money, if they had it, and often time and expertise as well. For instance, from its beginning, the Newcastle society had an honorary veterinary surgeon on its board and, in the early 1880s, a retired coroner did some prosecuting for them free of charge. The society also had certain legal powers, as will be shown.

Its first annual report began by saying that Newcastle had no reputation for gross brutality to animals. It continued:

> It is rare that instances of deliberate torture are brought under the notice of the Inspector, and no case of revolting cruelty, save one, where a woman was convicted of plucking a fowl alive, has been reported since the Society was established. Nearly all the offences hereabout consist in overloading and beating horses. The steep gradients leading from the lower to the upper parts of the town, and the roads in the suburbs, contiguous to landsale collieries, are the scenes of most of the cruelty which is practised in Newcastle... In Newcastle, the magistrates ordered eleven horses to be destroyed... it is known that upwards of a dozen wretched animals have been put out of their misery by their owners, to avoid the action of this Society.
>
> A considerable portion of the Inspector's time is occupied every Tuesday in Newcastle Cattle Market, where, from the intrusion of boys armed with sticks, animals suffer much torture, which the market keepers seem powerless to prevent. It has been suggested that the Corporation of Newcastle should give their officers authority to exclude these mischievous urchins, and that, at the same time, power should be obtained to issue licenses to drovers practising their calling here, so that some control may, as in London and elsewhere, be exercised over a somewhat callous and vagrant body of men.

It may be noted here that 'vagrant' at that time could be a word of insult as well as information. Vagrants were thought to have no sense of belonging anywhere, or, as we should say, no sense of community. But how the fact of being vagrant even in this sense should make them callous towards animals is not explained. It is possible that they were paid by results and by the hour:

the animals had to be in the market by such and such a time and how it was done was up to them. Some of the people arguing for better treatment of animals realised that it was wrong to blame a cruel practice on whichever person was last in a chain of command; the real fault lay with the original unfeasible order and the person who had issued it. 'Make bricks without straw!'

The first annual report carried directions for members of the public who wished to report cases of cruelty and these remained unchanged for decades:

> Any individual witnessing an act of cruelty, upon declaring his name and address to any police or other constable, can require the said constable to take the offender into custody, and forthwith convey him before a magistrate... Should no constable be present or near at hand, then the most advisable course is to report to... [the] Central Police Office, Newcastle-on-Tyne, who will undertake the prosecution of the offender at the Society's expense... The Society earnestly implores humane individuals not to be deterred from interference by a little personal trouble. A look from a bystander will sometimes save a blow; a word of reproach will generally do so.

Readers were assured that, by an Act of Parliament, all constables were bound to arrest anyone found being cruel to animals, upon being required to do so 'in the manner and form above-mentioned'.

The second annual report said that Mr Timperley, the inspector, 'has maintained a constant watch upon the cattle markets, fairs, and landing places, and upon the so-called local sports, which in many instances derive most of their interest from the terror and agony of dumb animals'. Prosecutions were brought by the police following information from Mr Timperley. Some offenders were gaoled; others were fined amounts ranging from £2 to £5 – a large sum for the times. The society, continues the report, sought prosecution only for deliberate cruelty, although it also provided education and assistance in avoiding thoughtless cruelty. Some examples of thoughtless cruelty were the bearing-rein on riding horses and the overloading of draught horses (referred to in an earlier section of this book).

One committee member claimed the instituting of the RSPCA had made a great difference to the amount of cruelty tolerated:

> A few years ago he used to stop boys and men who were abusing horses and cattle, and threaten them with all sorts of punishment. He even went to the extent of taking down their names, and threatening to prosecute personally; but he found it of little avail – all he received was abuse and contempt. But since the Society had opened a branch here he had noticed a marked difference. Not only was there much less cruelty, but cartmen and drovers paid more attention to private expostulations.

The report for 1875 noted fifty-four cases of cruelty to horses, three of ill-treatment of dogs and three of the torture of donkeys at Shields and Tynemouth. One owner of a deliberately starved donkey was gaoled for a month without the option of a fine. It was noted that the Agricultural Society in the Scottish Highlands taught its members how to treat livestock humanely; a wish was expressed that all agricultural societies would do the same. The scandal of the sale of worn-out pit ponies was brought up in this report (an incident which has been described in the 'Pit Ponies' section of the present book).

It was recommended that Inspector Timperley take up the matter of goats being left tethered to hedges with no shelter from the elements and unable to keep warm by moving around. One member had heard of five animals dying in one night in a neighbouring town (i.e. not Newcastle). But other members objected that untethered goats would cause damage.

The need to educate children, teaching them consideration for animals, was raised. The society itself had produced the *Humanity* series of six books for children, written by 'instruction through entertainment' and had donated a total of 700 volumes to Westmoreland Road Board School.

By 1876 Sunderland and Tynemouth had RSPCA organisations of their own, meaning that the Newcastle society could concentrate its efforts more locally. That year's annual report welcomed the *Newcastle Chronicle's* Dicky Bird Society: a children's club aiming to get children to be more considerate in such of their amusements as affected animals and birds and also to feed wild birds in winter.

A new inspector, Mr Warren, replaced Mr Timperley, who had been forced to retire to the warmer climate of Brighton, Newcastle being too cold for him. Mr Warren had been requested to examine slaughter methods in the town, some of which were felt to be very cruel.

Some delegates had been to an anti-vivisection conference in London where good arguments had been put forward, particularly by 'lady delegates'. It is interesting that in these years of the nineteenth century, vivisection was regarded by many as the ultimate in cruelty to animals and there was heated debate on the subject throughout the country. I suspect it was easier for most people to be strenuously anti-cruelty with regard to something they usually had no part in. It would have been much harder to examine and change their own lifelong habits in the matter of stagecoach horses, for instance.

Cruelty continued at livestock markets chiefly because the society had no legal power to license and inspect drovers. Even so, it was decreasing, as was the selling of worn-out pit ponies to pull carts.

The *Humanity* books produced by the society had been sent to more schools. The headmaster of one wrote: 'I am happy to say that the boys have given up robbing birds' nests, throwing stones at dogs, birds etc., which was once so common here.'

A speaker from London RSPCA, which was considered the parent society, had visited and addressed the Newcastle society. He praised its work but then went on mundanely to ask that it send more money to London in addition to the established £100 annual subscription. More importantly, this speaker brought up the question of who was originally the cause in any given case of cruelty. For instance, the overcrowding of cattle in a railway truck might not be the fault of the railway company but of the farmer who first loaded the animals on and who perhaps did not want to pay for extra trucks. The speaker ended with the heartening news that societies for the prevention of cruelty to animals were opening up throughout the world and were already well established in America.

The free distribution of the *Humanity* books to schools had to be stopped in 1877 as it was becoming too costly. The hope was that schools would buy the books instead: sadly, this proved a vain hope. But the *Chronicle* continued the good work of encouraging children to think about the lives of animals.

A plea was made for more observers at cattle markets to notice and report ill-treatment. (This same plea was made a few years ago, *c.* 2002, at the RSPCA's national headquarters. People are all very shocked when cattle are mistreated, but very few are willing or able to become unofficial inspectors.) It was recorded that the practice of driving and goading young calves – some almost newborn – through the streets, had been outlawed in London and soon would be, the committee hoped, in Newcastle. Also newly-forbidden in London was the marketing of shorn sheep in cold, wet weather. This would seem an unanswerable riposte to Mr Ellison's 'happy sheep' letter, quoted earlier in the present book. Bulls were still being dealt with cruelly, perhaps because there seemed no other way of handling big, dangerous animals. Imported bulls were unloaded from the ships roped together in fours, the ropes passing through rings in their noses. (I suspect that the 'bulls' described here were in fact castrated bullocks. I can think of no reason why entire males would be imported in large numbers.)

According to the 1879 report, a speaker from London had recommended that the Newcastle society set up a ladies' committee with its own secretary. It was felt that ladies would encourage subscriptions more successfully than men. They would bring in thousands of small subscriptions, all valuable not just for the money but as a means of raising people's awareness of the need for mercy and consideration towards animals. The London ladies' committee, said this speaker, put on regular entertainments for cab and tram drivers with the intention of teaching them merciful treatment of their horses. (Once again, one suspects that cab drivers would have been kinder to their horses had they not had to work to deadlines set by, often, the same ladies who sat on the committee.)

A Bill for the protection of wild birds was brought before Parliament but notoriously excluded landowners from its strictures, being aimed chiefly at 'bird-catchers', i.e. poor country people who caught and sold any wild birds they could. This was one case where the rich were privileged in law and the poor penalised. It does not show, however, that social control of the poor was its underlying motive. It was simply a case of injustice. People always defend their own practices and condemn those of others: in this case the rich were successful. In our own times of course the traditional hunting classes, threatened by legislation, have welcomed 'common' people into their pastimes – anything to defend the chase! This shows, I think, that the aim is to defend the pursuit, not to oppress the lower classes.

Despite the *Humanity* books, children were still tormenting animals at livestock markets and in the surrounding streets. Their favourite activities were beating the animals with sticks and setting their dogs on the sheep. I guess they did these things mindlessly because all their lives they had seen older children doing the same. By this date all children should have been in school on weekdays, but we know there was a lot of truancy in the first decades of the Compulsory Education Act. It would be a hundred years before British children arrived at the mindset they have today, one of thinking cruelty to animals the worst of evils.

Most perpetrators of cruelty in 1870s Newcastle were cautioned on the spot. Only egregious cases or repeat offenders were brought before a magistrate. It is notable that not all magistrates were sympathetic towards the RSPCA; some of them believed its activities to be a waste of money, inspired by tender feelings that would be better directed elsewhere.

By 1880 the police were helping to observe cattle markets and this brought about a marked drop in cases of cruelty. But there had been two cases of cruelty to pit ponies in mines; this was unusual as the ponies were usually well cared for.

Membership of the *Chronicle's* Dicky Bird Society now stood at 52,000. One committee member, Captain Blenkinsop-Coulson, brought up the subject of the cruelty practised regularly by the upper classes. One of the difficulties facing the RSPCA in its efforts to bring about more humane treatment of animals was 'the example. . . set to the young' by the 'squires, the ladies' and, he was sorry to say, 'even by parsons of parishes who took part in the pursuit after what they called "sport"; the only difference. . . being that whereas cruelty in the one case [i.e. that practised by children and poor people] was inflicted on domesticated animals, in the other it was inflicted upon wild animals'. Nor was Captain Coulson's the only upper-middle-class voice raised against blood sports in the nineteenth century. We may note ironically, however, that many of the hunting class were strong opponents of vivisection whilst defending their own cruel pastime with vigour.

The *Humanity* books had been offered half-price to board schools in Northumberland and Durham as well as Newcastle, but 'not one favourable reply was received', despite numerous recommendations. However, the London board schools had taken up the offer. The following year a possible solution to the cost of producing the books was proposed. All board schools had a financial allocation for books: if the society's series could be regarded as reading primers schools could obtain them with no additional expense. In effect, the government would be paying. The society was now producing a magazine as well as the books. *Animal World* was distributed free to schools and also to cab ranks and stables.

Addressing the committee, Captain Blenkinsop-Coulson wondered why no clergymen were members of Newcastle RSPCA. He proposed that an invitation be extended to the newly-installed first Bishop of Newcastle. Everyone on the committee agreed that 'Bishop Wilberforce would have joined'. His words must have had effect because one year later in 1882 the new Bishop of Newcastle had agreed to be the society's patron. Moreover, clergymen were beginning to join the various RSPCA societies. The Tynemouth society had the Revd A. Norris as its honorary secretary. In that society's annual report, the reverend had asserted that, 'the justices at Tynemouth strove to dispense justice independent of the position offenders might occupy in life'. It is clear that, much as the upper classes would have liked to escape animal-welfare measures, they were finding it harder and harder to do so. The Revd Norris also observed that companies were much harder to prosecute than individuals.

The captain then turned his attention to butchers. Much of the cruelty to animals destined to be meat, he claimed, resulted from butchers (who were slaughterers too) being drunk. We in the twenty-first century might feel like joining in his condemnation but should perhaps wonder whether we ourselves could go to work every day to kill dozens, if not hundreds, of animals without some kind of tranquilliser.

All the speakers at that year's annual general meeting (1882) urged lady members to do more by way of reporting cases and spreading the message of mercy and consideration. However there was no mention of a ladies' committee as suggested by the London speaker some years earlier.

The annual report for 1883 was the last one I could find for the nineteenth century. Since that year was also the society's tenth anniversary, the events and conclusions reported in this document stand as a sum of what had been achieved in ten years.

The unfortunate *Humanity* series could not after all be bought for schools out of their statutory book allowance as that fund did not cover books on the humane treatment of animals. The society decided finally to offer them as prizes in an essay competition to be held annually for all schools in Newcastle on the subject of 'Man's Duty to the Animals'. By 1883 five schools had shown an interest in the essay competition.

Amongst other things, this tenth annual report took the opportunity to review the progress of animal welfare over the whole country since the turn of the nineteenth century. It was pointed out that at that early date animals had had no legal standing but were simply property. Cruelty cases could be prosecuted but a conviction was only assured if it could be proved that the animal's owner had been harmed by what had been done to the animal – for instance, if a horse had been rendered too lame to pull its cart and the owner thus put in danger of losing his livelihood. In 1832 bull-baiting, dog-fights and cockfights had been banned in London under a bye-law, but an attempt three years later to apply the prohibition countrywide had been met with ferocious opposition. Nevertheless, bye-laws were passed area by area, including one in Newcastle forbidding bull-baiting. (I cannot help wondering whether bull-baiting has ever been popular in Newcastle. Eighteenth- and nineteenth-century newspapers here carried no notices of it although, as we have seen, they did advertise cockfighting.)

By the date of this anniversary report – 1883 – there were 300 RSPCA societies in the United Kingdom with seventy sister societies in Europe and the USA. In addition, by this time nearly all towns and even villages had drinking troughs for horses. The transport of livestock was much more humane; ironically this had come about as a result of hygiene requirements following repeated outbreaks of cattle disease. The docking of horses' tails had been condemned by lead veterinary surgeons but was not yet illegal and so many owners still practised it. Thomas Nelson, the Sheriff of Newcastle, made a contribution to the report in which he said: 'The Society [RSPCA]... in raising its voice against cruelty... left no class or sect untouched... There were the vicious sports of the rich; there were the low vicious sports among the poor.'

The next available RSPCA annual report was for 1938 – over half a century later. What took place in the society during those years must remain, as far as this book is concerned, unknown. Fortunately, other sources enable us to piece together the progress of animal welfare in Newcastle during the 'missing' years; we now take up the RSPCA annual report for 1938.

The society now had a regular clinic in New Bridge Street with free treatment for sick and injured animals on two afternoons and one evening per week. The fact of one evening opening shows, I think, thoughtfulness towards working people who would not have been able to take time off work to see to their sick animals. Generous donations and subscriptions made free treatment possible and animals' owners were asked to make a donation of whatever amount they could afford. The society also operated an animal refuge in Gateshead; this was a boarding kennel to answer the problem of owners turning their animals on to the streets when they went away for any reason. The annual report of 1938 says:

> The Committee do earnestly appeal to animal lovers to help by reporting cases of cruelty immediately. With only three Inspectors for a very large and thickly populated area, the Committee would greatly appreciate the cooperation of the public. It is not necessary for ladies or gentlemen to interfere personally if they do not wish to do so. . . if the name and number on a cart are reported to the Branch Office. . . the Inspector will examine the animal and take appropriate action.
>
> Information is treated as strictly confidential, but for obvious reasons the Society cannot undertake to investigate anonymous complaints. The Committee also ask that cases of cruelty which are only hearsay should not be reported unless accompanied by the name and address of some person who can give first-hand information.

The annual essay competition for schools, begun in the 1880s and offering the society's own books as prizes, was now an established feature of school life in Newcastle with many children sending in entries. It was reported that both Tynemouth and Gateshead councils had been approached by their local RSPCA branches to adopt humane slaughter methods. Both had agreed but refused to include sheep. However, individual wards in both towns could include sheep if they wished and some had voted to do so. Newcastle RSPCA now had a Tailwaggers' Club which paid the statutory dog-licence fees for people who could not afford to pay but who were good owners.

At this time, many animal-welfare Bills were before Parliament including: (1) the prohibition of 'carted' stag hunting [presumably the carting of a stag to suitable moorland where hounds could hunt the animal], (2) the prohibition of owning birds or accoutrements for cockfighting, (3) one to outlaw the hunting of wild deer with hounds and (4) another to outlaw vivisection on dogs. (We may note that not until the beginning of the twenty-first century was the hunting of wild deer with hounds made illegal and vivisection on dogs is still permitted, albeit under strict controls.) Other proposed measures included improving working conditions for pit ponies. The abuses addressed in these Bills were found throughout the United Kingdom as a whole; in calling attention to them, the society was not suggesting Newcastle itself was particularly at fault.

One of the three inspectors, Mr Hamilton, reported that treatment of animals at markets in Newcastle was generally good, but that constant supervision was necessary. (We see here the unmistakeably positive influence of over sixty years of RSPCA presence.)

The next available annual report was for 1969. For the first time, this report mentioned seabirds mired in oil slicks along the coast: some had been successfully cleaned and returned to the wild but many, too badly affected, had had to be humanely destroyed. Inspector Mossop also drew attention to the numbers of stray dogs killed by traffic, dogs mostly without collars or registration. (The date – 1969 – suggests dogs left homeless as a result of slum clearance.)

By 1970 the clinic had moved from New Bridge Street to Shields Road. There was the problem of numerous stray cats; the society was offering to neuter pet cats of either sex at reduced rates to prevent the proliferation of unwanted kittens. Inspector Mossop said, 'during the year I investigated seventy-three complaints, in the course of which I was assaulted and sustained relatively minor but nonetheless painful injuries. . . I made two rescues, one involving three cows trapped under forty tons of oats in a collapsed barn'. Additional clinics had been opened at Bedlington and North Shields.

The last RSPCA annual report I saw was for 1971. Here the chairman's statement sounded a note of exasperation. It seemed people no longer felt grateful for the society but simply took it for granted. (This must be, I think, the fate of any bold and compassionate initiative when it has been in existence many decades. Generations of people grow up never knowing what things were like before.) To quote the chairman:

Some owners even consider it their right that all responsibility such as veterinary attention, removal of unwanted litters and even spaying should be handled by the RSPCA. [This seems an odd complaint considering the society was offering cut-price spaying the previous year.] 'Local Government Offices also appear to expect this charity to be able to deal with animals' problems created by our modern society, such as colonies of stray cats and packs of dogs, without lending support either financial or by acknowledging the various problems and taking active steps to combat them...

One of the inspectors told how oil-slick contamination and the resulting deaths of seabirds had continued, despite pressure from conservationists and government agencies. (The fact that conservationists and government agencies were trying to do something about the evil rather contradicts the chairman's statement that the public expected the RSPCA to do everything.)

Many animals had been re-homed, including a fox! Several dogs had been pulled out of the ground or pits; sadly not all had survived. A bullock had been rescued from a cesspit, and a pony from a bog, with the help of Alnwick fire brigade. Enquiries and visitors had come from many countries and one specific case of cruelty investigated by the inspector had originated in Norway!

No further annual reports of Newcastle RSPCA were available to me. In any case, dates later than 1970 are within living memory for most people and it was not my intention to bring this history right up to the present day. Other animal-welfare organisations came into being in nineteenth- and early twentieth-century Newcastle, as we shall see...

Newcastle PDSA

The People's Dispensary for Sick Animals began in the East End of London in 1917; like the RSPCA it was a completely charitable concern. Its founder, Maria Dickin, was concerned that very poor people could not afford either the time or money to take their sick animals to a vet and although by that time the RSPCA had established some clinics, these were not numerous enough to be within reach for many people. She therefore equipped a travelling veterinary surgery in addition to her clinic in an East End basement. Within a few years, the number of surgery vans expanded and so did the idea of providing easily attainable medical care for animals belonging to poor people.

Newcastle's PDSA clinic opened in 1950 in Westmoreland Road, one of its first patients being a cat with a darning needle stuck in its throat! Like the RSPCA, the PDSA asked for donations from people whose animals it treated if they could afford it. Some who could not afford it offered to scrub floors or do other odd jobs instead. One year a playwright and a cast of actors appearing at the Theatre Royal rescued a number of stray cats and took them to the PDSA. (As we have seen, stray cats were a huge problem in the mid-twentieth century due to slum clearance and re-housing.) By 1953 there were four PDSA clinics in the Tyne and Wear area treating a total of 1,000 pets per week. The PDSA's area of operation was simply veterinary treatment, unlike the RSPCA which concerned itself with detecting, reporting and prosecuting cruelty to animals as well.

An article in the *Chronicle* in 1953 reported that the PDSA had treated an Australian blue-tongued skink – certainly its most exotic patient up to that date!

Newcastle upon Tyne Dog and Cat Shelter

This shelter was founded in 1895 on the same site where it stands today at the very top of Claremont Road. It was and still is a charitable enterprise with a remit to take in and care for homeless, injured and unwanted animals. I can do no better than to quote from its own leaflet issued in the 1970s as part of an appeal for funds to complete the building of an extension:

> Under an agreement with the police, all stray dogs in Newcastle, Gateshead, Gosforth and some outlying districts of Co. Durham are taken in and cared for at the shelter. In one year alone, some two thousand dogs are received and, of these, homes are found for over 60 per cent…
>
> With the exception of a small fee from the Newcastle and Northumberland Police Authorities, the Shelter is maintained entirely from voluntary subscriptions, donations and boarding fees…
>
> All the kennels are large and airy and the feeding and general care of the animals is unequalled. In addition, all animals in the Shelter are regularly examined by our veterinary surgeons…
>
> The Shelter Boarding Service has been the subject of many congratulations… from those who have made use of it and you may rest assured that dogs and cats boarded at our establishment receive the best care and attention that can be given to them.

The fact that people in the twentieth century were starting to board out their animals showed a change from the past. In earlier times it had been quite common practice to leave dogs and cats to fend for themselves when owners went away for any reason. They were shut out of the house and left to get on with things as best they could. It is easy with hindsight to blame people for doing this but the owners involved often had very grave worries about their children, their money, their jobs and their elderly relatives, as well as probably being poor and not in good health. They simply did not have any compassion left to cover their animals as well. Besides, they did their best for them when they were at home. Many people lived with a degree of hardship unimaginable to us.

Another not-uncommon practice was to leave pet animals behind when moving house – a practice notoriously contributed to by town councils with their slum-clearance programmes. Very often, animals were not allowed in the new houses or flats where people were moving. This abandonment resulted, of course, in large numbers of stray dogs and even larger numbers of cats, some of which turned feral and bred without restraint. The possibility of having a pet dog or cat boarded or, in exceptional circumstances, re-homed, must have been a comfort to at least some of the people moving to a desirable new home which unfortunately did not welcome their animals.

The Dicky Bird Society

This society, which enjoyed huge success with children countrywide and even worldwide during the late nineteenth and early twentieth centuries, was the creation of W.E. Adams, author of *Children's Corner* in the *Newcastle Chronicle*. Adams wanted to make the children of Newcastle aware of the lives of the wild birds which were so often the target of boys' cruel sports. Although birds were his primary object of interest, other species were also included in the aim. Begun on the 7 October 1876, the society defined itself as being, 'for the promotion of kindness towards birds and all living things'.

Typically for the time, Adams gave himself a sentimental pen name, 'Uncle Toby', and claimed to be being advised by an ancient bird called 'Father Chirpie'. In choosing 'Uncle Toby', Adams revealed he had been inspired by the eponymous character in *Tristram Shandy* who released an annoying bluebottle out of the window rather than killing it. A coloured plate which served as the logo of the society was available to members. To modern eyes it is cloying and un-lifelike, showing 'Uncle Toby' surrounded by five handsome and pretty children – one of whom is perched on his knee – with 'Father Chirpie' balancing on the chair back. Four of the children are clearly middle class and well dressed, but the fifth is a little maidservant wearing a plain dress and a mobcap. We must bear in mind that the same level of sentimental make-believe operates today in Disneyland and in the character of Ronald McDonald.

On applying to join, children signed a pledge which read: 'I hereby promise to be kind to all Living things, to protect them to the utmost of my power; and never to take or destroy Birds' Nests. I also promise to get as many Boys and Girls as possible to join the Dicky Bird Society.' At the time, collecting birds' eggs to make complete collections was a popular pastime for boys and approved by adults as somewhat scientific – an altogether healthy occupation. 'Uncle Toby' was equivocal on the subject: he asked boys who joined the Dicky Bird Society to sign an additional pledge promising never to take more than one egg from any nest. It was soon pointed out that if every boy took just one egg from every nest, the result would be no eggs in any nest. 'Uncle Toby' tried to explain his position in a reply sent to one of the adult critics: if he condemned the hobby out of hand, many boys would be put off joining the society and therefore not consider birds' lives at all. In movements such as his, he explained, it was better to take one step at a time.

A 'sport' much worse had been witnessed by 'Uncle Toby' himself in an (unnamed) pit village. Some boys had tied up a bird then laid it down in front of a wall – wings and legs fastened together – and stoned it to death. He very much hoped to gain some Dicky Bird Society members in that village.

Temperance festival, 1938: smart pony and young rider.

There were grades of membership in the society: 'captains' and 'companions'. Some references suggest these indicated boy and girl members respectively. Children who joined were encouraged to write to the *Chronicle* with news, poems and anecdotes about animals. Great numbers responded and many of their letters were reproduced verbatim in the paper's *Children's Corner*. Many described how the young writers took care to feed wild birds, especially in winter when birds' usual food was not available. The winter of 1886 was particularly hard, with deep snow, but boys and girls cleared their yards and put out food for the birds. The modern reader is astonished at the literacy and almost-correct grammar of these letters from seven- and eight-year-olds. What moves us in another, heartbreaking way, are the weekly, sometimes daily, reports of the deaths of the little society members. Children whose letters and poems were published one week were often dead the next and sensitively mourned in 'Uncle Toby's' editorials. The killers would have been measles, scarlet fever, diphtheria, TB and all the infectious diseases of childhood so rare today.

Some boys wrote in proudly that they had beaten up other boys having caught them tormenting birds and this was approved by 'Uncle Toby,' though he suggested spreading the word as well!

From time to time children were invited to decorate the envelopes they sent their letters in. These designs were reproduced in the paper; once again they excite present-day admiration for the skill they show, although it is possible that parents helped. One showed 'Father Chirpie' berating a fashionable lady for the 'borrowed plumes' in her hat. All elements in that picture are well-drawn: the bird, the lady and the hat.

The appeal of the Dicky Bird Society spread countrywide as North-Eastern children wrote to their cousins and friends in other parts of the country. Soon there were members all over the United Kingdom; other local newspapers were quick to follow the lead and start up similar children's clubs of their own. But the original Dicky Bird Society remained the most popular and over the years even gained members in other countries. In 1886 'Uncle Toby' received a letter from a Russian boy written in Cyrillic script saying he had become a member of a DBS affiliated society. The *Chronicle* printed the letter unchanged. Another letter from a South African member in 1886 described a strange 'bird' the writer had seen with a 'mouse's face': almost certainly this would have been a bat. Occasionally adults wrote in to the society, apologising for their age but eager to recount some animal anecdote of their own.

The *Daily News*, a London-based national paper, reported on 27 July 1886 that:

> ... the Dicky Bird Society is composed primarily of the boys and girls of Newcastle; secondly, of the boys and girls of the civilized world. It is a society for the promotion of kindness to animals, which is much better as an active stimulus to exertion than the mere prevention of cruelty...

By 1886 worldwide membership had reached 100,000 and by 1894 a quarter of a million! 1886 was a great year for the society. For the tenth anniversary of its founding, the society held a celebratory festival and demonstration in the Tyne Theatre. Buns, fruits, sweets and water were laid on for the children and an audience of 4,000 attended despite atrocious weather. Professional singers, musicians and entertainers gave their services free, but by far the most popular attraction was the singing and music made by the children themselves. The festival was widely reported in national and local newspapers, including the island of Jersey's *Observer*. All critics agreed (though who, indeed, would disagree?) that the children's performances had been excellent.

The Dicky Bird Society's example spread to adults as well. In this regard we must bear in mind that in all ages there have been some compassionate men and women, whatever the behaviour of the wider society. One child member of the DBS wrote from Kent telling of a farmer who had reproved some boys for bird's-nesting. Normally farmers and country people in general had harder hearts towards animals and birds than city dwellers. But news also came of a farmer close at hand in Seaton Delaval who, whilst cutting a field of wheat, had found about twenty peewits' nests. He had carefully removed them until all the cutting was finished and then replaced them. Some other farmers though took the more usual view and encouraged boys to stone birds in the wheat fields with catapults. Children wrote in to the society complaining that their efforts to save birds by feeding them had been thwarted: boys waited until the birds settled near the food and then attacked them, spurred on by the farmers. Some of the farmers gathered up the dead birds to feed them to their cats.

As we have seen, for many centuries cats were regarded equivocally. But certainly the late nineteenth-century children in the Dicky Bird Society loved their pet cats, even, according to one letter, petting them until they cried. The little girl explained that she could not help doing this, she loved them so. At the same time, the society recognised that cats were the chief persecutors of birds. 'Uncle Toby' advised putting a small bell on a collar around every cat's neck; this advice continues to the present day so far as I know. Boys who were not members of the DBS often beat and tortured cats unmercifully, sometimes giving as their rationale the cats' habit of attacking birds. It is doubtful that this was their true motive.

To celebrate the worldwide membership of 250,000 recorded in 1894, a grand commemoration was held in the recreation ground on Town Moor.

I could find no record of the Dicky Bird Society later than 1894 and have no idea what became of it. It is possible that as the idea of compassion to birds and animals spread over the whole of society there was less need for the DBS. A more mundane possibility is that W.E. Adams ('Uncle Toby') retired, or even died, and that no one else could be found to continue the society.

The Progress of Animal-Welfare Legislation

We have already noted that for most of human history animals were regarded as no more than the possessions of whoever owned or caught them. Any 'offence' committed against an animal, including birds, could only be considered illegal if it prejudiced the owner's wellbeing in some way. There have always been animal doctors of one sort or another: for instance, much doctoring of horses was done by farriers. But the aim was simply to restore the animals to working capability. The first veterinary colleges in the United Kingdom were established in London in 1791 and Edinburgh in 1823, both being granted the royal charter in 1844. Once again though, this did not necessarily imply a merciful attitude towards animals; it only answered the need of their owners for their valuable animals to be fit to work, give milk or whatever. From 1866 only those qualified by one of the royal colleges were permitted to call themselves veterinary surgeons.

However there have always been people who think that animals, being capable of experiencing pain and suffering, should be afforded some protection from cruel treatment. By the early nineteenth century there was a lobby for a measure of protection for certain domestic animals, including where necessary protection from their owners. 1823 saw the passing of an Act of Parliament to penalise cruel and improper treatment of cattle, an Act which was expanded two years later. During the sixty years from 1849-1909, a number of Cruelty to Animals Acts were passed, each widening the definition of cruelty and including more species, although in some cases owners and handlers were given sympathetic consideration. For instance, an Act of 1875 made the doping of racehorses illegal. Probably it was thought that horses should not be whipped to win a race when they had been previously doped to make this impossible. But equally probably the interests of the owners, trainers and gamblers were paramount. Similarly, 1883 saw an Act extending the existing regulations of dairies, cowsheds and milk shops. It is possible some clauses of this Act referred to the cows' own wellbeing, but we can be sure the main purpose was to safeguard human health.

As we have seen, dog licences were introduced by Queen Victoria's government in 1867, the details of which have been given elsewhere in this book.

Unsuccessful Bills against: (1) cruelty and abuse in vivisection and (2) the practice of vivisection itself were put forward in 1881 and 1883. The anti-vivisection movement was strong and popular. People wanted to consider themselves humane, but they did not want to give up those practices on which their own daily welfare depended, such as whipping and overloading horses. Opposing vivisection gave them the perfect opportunity to feel compassionate without actually changing their ways.

The Protection of Animals Act of 1911 gathered previous legislation into one document and clarified it. This Act, although added to, altered in details and subsumed under later Acts, remains the bedrock of animal cruelty law. It defined cruel actions and made them illegal, and put an onus on owners, trainers and handlers to avoid the passive cruelty of neglect. Besides mammals it covered all domesticated birds and one or two other species. Owners or handlers were made liable for acts of cruelty committed by others if at the time the animal was nominally in their care. Its main provisions were:

1. It was an offence to cruelly beat, kick, over-ride, over-drive, overload, torture, infuriate or terrify any animal. 'Cruelly' meant 'so as to cause unnecessary suffering'. Some practices, such as the dehorning of cattle, did cause pain but were unavoidable if a farmer was to control his animals; they were therefore exempt. But painless procedures, if available, were always to be preferred to painful ones, even if the painless alternatives were expensive or troublesome.

2. It was an offence to fail to provide food, water, shelter, medical care etc. for an animal in one's care. To neglect this, even through thoughtlessness, was a punishable offence. People should not acquire animals without taking into account the responsibilities incurred.

3. It was an offence to convey animals in such a way as to cause suffering, or to order that this be done. Here finally is acknowledgement that the perpetrator of a cruel act might well not be the one to blame if he was simply carrying out the orders on which his livelihood depended.

4. 'Fighting or baiting' of any animal, plus the accessories to such activities, was forbidden. Bull-baiting had long been illegal; this paragraph must therefore have applied to dog-fights. It seems not to have applied to cockfights which were not officially banned until after the Second World War, despite having fallen into unpopularity.

5. Poisoning or drugging any animal without good cause was outlawed. Moles, rats and squirrels could be poisoned but not with certain prohibited poisons.

6. It was an offence to perform any surgery on an animal without due care and humanity (this usually meant anaesthesia), with certain exceptions, such as licensed research, dehorning of cattle and castration.

7. Abandonment of domestic animals was an offence.

8. Dogs were not to be used as draught animals. (This last directive strikes us as quaint and also hardly necessary as dogs were never widely used to pull carts in this country although they were in some others.)

The penalties for conviction of cruelty were up to six months' imprisonment or a fine and sometimes both. Over time the possible fine increased so that by 1989 the maximum was £2,000. Ill-treated animals could be taken away from the owner and either re-homed or, if a vet advised it, humanely destroyed. If the misused animal was a dog then the convicted person was banned from ever keeping a dog again.

We have already noted the Coal Mines Act, also passed in 1911, which afforded extra protection for horse and pit ponies.

In 1901 a Bill was put before Parliament to make it an offence to 'contaminate' horses' public drinking troughs; it did not become law. We may wonder what the 'contamination' was – urine? General rubbish? A trough would have been a convenient dump for both. But we must remember that at that time public toilets were widely provided; as for rubbish, domestic middens were cleared at least once a week, sometimes nightly.

The years 1906-9 saw Bills being put forward against 'spurious sports'. Those tendering the Bills hoped to include fox- and stag-hunting in their remit, but their main aim was those 'sports' where animals were enclosed for the purpose of being shot or killed by dogs. The most egregious example of this, I suppose, would be shooting fish in a barrel and the most hallowed, the royal deer parks. In 1921 an Act, successful this time, prohibited the shooting of captive birds. Perhaps it was this Act which ended the pigeon shooting which had been so popular in Newcastle, as elsewhere.

An Act of 1900 extended some legal protection to wild birds, including the introduction of a 'close season' for hunted birds. Another Act of 1908 forbade the importation of plumage for decorating hats.

The first Bill to make humane slaughter the only acceptable method was put forward in 1914 but did not become law for more than a decade, although civic authorities were empowered to write it into their bye-laws. As we have seen, the humane method was adopted in Newcastle in the 1920s.

In 1921 a Bill was put forward trying to outlaw performing animals and menageries; it was not successful. Music-hall acts with performing dogs remained popular, certainly in Newcastle, until well after the Second World War; so did animals in circuses.

In 1932 came a Bill and subsequently an Act to licence dog-racing courses. Newcastle's Brough Park Greyhound Stadium then came into its own.

Arguments For and Against Compassion to Animals

Eighteenth-century England – so civilised, so creative, in such intellectual ferment – was, in its day-to-day habits, often brutal and unfeeling. Public hangings were a popular spectacle, poverty was thought incurable and the church, once the conscience of the people, had lost much of its authority on account of memories of the religious wars that had devastated the preceding centuries. *Laissez-faire* was the order of the day: leave people and their habits alone, concentrating energy rather on the wonderful new discoveries of science and mechanics. If people were cruel to children and animals (and to each other for that matter), then that was just the way the world was. But, as always, there were dissenting voices.

In 1802 a Member of Parliament, Percival Stockdale, wrote a 'Remonstrance Against Inhumanity to Animals and Particularly Against the Savage Practice of Bull-Baiting'. He quoted a letter he had received describing a bull-baiting in Bury St Edmunds: 'The chief magistrate used every exertion to prevent its being carried into execution, but in vain, and the poor animal was tortured and dragged through the streets of the town, according to annual custom.'

The Bury St Edmunds case was far from the worst. In some places the bull's feet were cut off to prevent his escape should he break free, his horns sawn down to the quick to torture and enrage him and gunpowder lit in front of his face as he lay dying to try to get an extra drop of 'game' from him.

The horrors of bull-baiting were being exposed at the same time as the horrors of the slave-trade: indeed Mr Stockdale's Remonstrance appeared in a pamphlet appealing for the abolition of the slave trade. How, it was asked, could a country either Christian or civilised, still less one claiming to be both, allow such practices? The 'Remonstrance', written it seems from the point of view of deism rather than revivalist Christianity, declared:

> It cannot be disputed that universal humanity is an essential part of both natural and revealed religion. . .
> [T]his humanity must attentively extend to the animal creation. It is our evident, and indispensable
> duty not to give them any wanton or unnecessary pain; but if we exercise our ingenuity in making
> their torment our sport; by provoking their natural instinct of self-defence to rage, and madness; to
> the destruction of one another; if we eagerly stimulate brutal fierceness (which, while we excite it, we
> emulate) to exasperate their agony; we are guilty of most barbarous impiety. . . We are told. . . that these
> diversions of blood and riot make their disciples brave, generous and heroick. The reverse of this. . . is
> the fact. They naturally, and generally, make them cowardly, ferocious and abandoned.

Mr Stockdale mounted his chief attack against the aristocracy, writing that 'persons in elevated stations... who, by a bright variety of enjoyments; by a flowery and exhilarating road through life, seem to be wooed and intreated by Providence to be humane, generous, friendly,' in fact show 'pride, selfishness and oppression... [T]hey act as if they imagined that they and the inferior orders of men, were framed with different natural sensations and sentiments; that all their exquisite feelings are expended on themselves'. Still less did such people consider the feelings of other species. He then made a link between heartlessness towards one's fellow men and cruelty to animals by turning his fire on the chief supporter of the continuance for bull-baiting. He did not name the man, but other MPs knew well who was meant:

> The Gentleman who has the honour to be the principal patron of this abominable sport [bull-baiting]... has maintained a consistent hardness and inflexibility in his philosophy on very important occasions... He has viewed the ravages of war; the destruction of our species; the miseries of mankind, with a perfect apathy... We need not wonder that he sees nothing horrible, and detestable in bull-baiting...

The arguments of those who wished to retain the sport were: (1) bull-baiting was a trifling matter not worth Parliament's consideration and (2) it was a venerable and hallowed tradition. But the chief argument of those opposing all animal-welfare measures was that, in the Book of Genesis, God had delivered the beasts of the field, fowls of the air and fish of the sea into Adam's hands to do with as he pleased. However, in the 1830s Lord Justice Hales, dealing with a reported cruelty case, laid down that, although God had made man 'lord' of creation, He had not made him its tyrant.

At the time of Mr Stockdale's Bill, Newcastle was, as far as I can discover, entirely free of bull-baiting as a recognised sport (although bulls and other livestock going to market were regularly tormented by children), as was the whole of Scotland. Certainly such issues of the *Chronicle* for the late eighteenth and early nineteenth centuries as I have been able to find have no reports of bull-baiting. By contrast, Ireland had a bad reputation for animal cruelty. Bull-baiting was popular there, the bulls being sometimes half-flayed alive, i.e. the skin pulled off the head and shoulders to increase pain and rage.

In 1839 a Mr Youatt, a native of the North East, wrote an essay on 'The Obligation and Extent of Humanity to Brutes, Principally Concerned with Reference to the Domesticated Animals'. He offered the essay to the newly-formed Society for the Prevention of Cruelty (not yet 'to animals' and not yet 'royal'), but they did not publish it. It deserves to be quoted:

> At no very distant period, the right of wantonly torturing the inferior animals, as caprice or passion dictated, was unblushingly claimed; and it was asserted that the prevention of this was an interference with the rights and liberties of man!!

(We may note that, since the rights of man rather than the rights of kings, seigneurs etc. was a passionate and novel topic for the time, this was quite a strong argument. This early example shows up the conflict between the ideals of liberty and compassion: free people are free to be cruel and therefore if cruelty is to be stopped it requires taking away the freedom of some people. We see a similar conflict in our own times between the ideals of tolerance and democracy: if everything is to be tolerated, nothing can be condemned as undemocratic and intolerance itself has to be tolerated.)

Returning to Mr Youatt's essay, he gave examples from Scripture where mercy to animals was enjoined. For instance, Solomon stated that a righteous man cares for his beasts but a wicked man has no feeling for them. These Scriptural examples went against official Church teaching, which was that the beasts were entirely for man's use and pleasure. Mr Youatt told a charming story about animals in classical Athens:

The people... when they had finished the temple called Hecatompedon, set at liberty the beasts of burden that had chiefly been employed in that work, suffering them to pasture at large, free from any further service. It is said that one of these afterwards came of its own accord to work and, putting itself at the head of the labouring cattle, marched before them into the citadel. This pleased the people; and they made a decree that it should be kept at the public charge as long as it lived.

Still drawing on antiquity, the author said chariot-race horses were pensioned off when old and so were farm draught animals. This contrasted with the present-day (for the author) English practice of frequently slaughtering worn-out animals. Besides classical, Judaean and Christian sources, he quoted from other scriptures in an attempt to show that the deepest thinkers in all traditions preached compassion towards animals.

As we have seen, the subject of cruelty to animals had been coming up in Parliament since the beginning of the nineteenth century and Lord Erskine's Bill of 1802 provoked continuing debate for decades. Starting with the 1823 Act which afforded some protection to cattle, the tide of feeling began to turn in favour of compassion and in the half-century beginning 1849 more and more anti-cruelty legislation was passed. From then on those who wished to retain certain questionable practise had to argue that they were not cruel; they could no longer argue that cruelty did not matter.

Sometimes it was argued that although practice x might be cruel it only happened occasionally and was in any case the price to be paid for some great good. Discussion became about details. One speaker for instance, answering Mr Youatt's recommendations, advocated the slaughter of worn-out animals if they could not be pensioned off comfortably but would be liable to starve or freeze. Some speakers defended fox-hunting and deer-stalking (which they no doubt practised themselves), arguing that they were not cruel, whilst seeking to have other blood sports abolished. An interesting recurrent excuse for some activities was that 'manly sports' (hunting, hare coursing, dog-fighting etc.) might occasionally lead a 'gentleman' to be cruel, but that this should be tolerated in the interest of 'manliness'! Habitual cruelty, said these apologists, was a different matter and should always be condemned. Needless to say, the question of where occasional cruelty ended and habitual began was not addressed and nor was the question of whose judgment should be called on.

The hardest fact for all to face was the involvement of the general public in cruelty, usually through thoughtlessness. At the beginning of the century, Lord Erskine himself had graphically described the fate of old horses: pack horses worked to death, sinking and dying in harness under intolerable loads and stagecoach horses grown useless with non-stop work, left to starve in knackers' yards. Yet everyone wanted their own journeys to be quick and their own goods delivered on time. Lord Erskine also drew attention, as we have seen, to the mistake of blaming servants or other menials for animals' suffering at their hands when, in fact, they had been merely carrying out cruel and impracticable orders.

The question arose of how anti-cruelty laws could be carried out, especially as regards cruelty committed by the upper classes. Said one speaker: '... Few would inform against his worship the squire because he had rode his hunter to death, or unmercifully whipped, or in a fit of passion shot, his pointer.' The livelihood of anyone who so 'informed' would immediately be in jeopardy. As for accusations of cruelty against the lower orders, false and mischievous accusations would be made one against the other to settle old scores. This would happen even if no reward were offered for information; if such a reward were offered the bringing of accusations would increase a hundredfold.

One speaker spelled out the universal but usually unmentioned difference between theory and practice. Upper-class ladies often called for laws against cruelty to animals, but when it was pointed out that this would mean their 'wonderful' coachman not getting them from a to b quite so quickly, they lost their zeal. It was rank hypocrisy to demand anti-cruelty legislation on the one hand and insist that one's own horses 'do nine miles an hour because I am in a hurry' on the other. The speaker continued:

Where was the justice of punishing an innkeeper [licensed to hire out horses] who, if he had refused [to hire out] his horses [because they were already tired out or sick] lost his customers and his means of livelihood; or the post-boy, who, when once employed, must perform the task assigned to him by such means as he had, and must ply the whip till the pain and threat overcame the pain of the effort, which was requisite to carry the horses through their stage?

We can see that long before animal-welfare legislation began to be passed many people already felt cruel practices were wrong and should not be tolerated. The 'Genesis' or Church view of animals was losing favour: other species were no longer seen merely as food, labour or sport for humans. But there was some cultural distance to go between this position and actual Parliamentary legislation against cruelty. During this interregnum the view prevailed that cruelty to animals was a moral wrong but should not be subject to the law any more than other moral wrongs like fury, gluttony and the rest of the once-deadly sins. It was taken as axiomatic throughout the whole period (except by a few eccentric philosophers) that human welfare must always override animal welfare where the two were in conflict. The arguments were about what was included in 'human welfare'; in particular were human whim, caprice or wish for amusement to be admitted, or the desire to make boys 'manly'? There was no general notion of animal rights; what was invoked was the human duty of compassion.

Conclusion, Including Three Bears

Many of the theoretical conclusions to be drawn from this short overview have emerged in the course of the story. What remains is to counter the charge made in Harriet Ritvo's book that nineteenth-century animal-welfare reforms were really a covert means of social control of the poor by the rich. Certainly the rich fought hard to defend their privileged pastimes but they often defended lower-class cruel sports like bull-baiting just as vigorously. Equally certainly the ruling classes wanted to keep the whip hand over the rest of society and were very much afraid of new legislation enfranchising some of the lower orders. But it is stretching credibility to say they used animal-welfare measures as an attempt to keep their old control. Yes, those of the upper classes who opposed cruelty used sneering language when describing the cruel practices of the poor. But this, I would contend is simply an example of the universal tendency to condemn others' faults whilst tolerating the same faults in oneself. The enemy that the ruling classes fought against was not so much the lower classes as the new spirit. They did not want their comfortable old habits challenged at every turn. Neither, for that matter, did the poor, except when it was in their interest. At the same time the appeal of the new spirit was felt: it was the 'modern' thing to do to express compassion. But everyone, rich and poor alike, was guilty of not matching what they did to what they said – a fault which is probably a part of human nature. The tendency to keep doing the same thing no matter what one professes checks progress always and everywhere. In order for wicked practices to stop more is needed than declarations of outrage or even the passing of laws.

I end on a lighter note with some anecdotes from the years immediately before and after 1950: all courtesy of the *Chronicle* archives.

A pet magpie that smoked was reported at Whickham. The bird had learned to smoke accidentally by continually picking up its owner's lighted cigarettes and become hooked.

A tropical species of kingfisher was regularly sighted in Jesmond Dene.

In 1950 an albatross was seen by several people in Osborne Road.

A music-hall double act put on in 1953 featured a chimpanzee, William, as one half of the duo. When the other (human) half was taken ill, William performed solo and pleased all audiences.

The year 1954 saw an early appearance of the young Barbara Woodhouse, riding a cow called Snow Queen alongside her daughter on a pony.

The next year an antlered stag swam up the Tyne pursued by a police launch. It was caught and handed over to the RSPCA.

Barnum & Bailey
circus elephant
passing the Theatre
Royal, 1898.

There were reports of a pack of foxes (very unusual) killing hundreds of poultry at Wrekenton. A retired miner shot them all.

Private animal sanctuaries began springing up in the city including an animal boarding house in Dispensary Lane run by Mr John Speers.

A baby baboon brought home as a pet by a merchant seaman as a present for Mrs Clarkson and her five children escaped one morning, attracting large crowds. It bit a woman but was captured by the RSPCA.

Free dog licences for pensioners were proposed in 1958. (As we know, a decade later dog licences were done away with.)

In 1958 a number of exotic animals were landed at Newcastle Quay, among them chimpanzees,

Barnum & Bailey circus procession, 1898.

lynxes and pythons. (We are not told who ordered the animals; nowadays a special government licence would be required.)

There was said to be a 'constant problem' of deer running around the outskirts of the city. Also in 1958 the Newcastle Dog and Cat Shelter held a Christmas party for dogs, which was a great success; it was decided to hold one every year.

In 1960 a Himalayan pet bear named Bobby was leaving his home (a pet shop in Clayton Street) for a new home in Edinburgh. It seems he was going to the right place as he loved porridge!

In the same year Mr Tom Murphy rescued an injured hare from Newcastle Gold Club; ever since it followed him round like a pet dog.

In 1963 a fox cub which had been made an orphan by hounds was reared by a pet cat which had lost two kittens.

Also in 1963 came reports of a steeple-chasing nanny goat! She had been born in the stables at Kenton riding school and became close friends with a foal born there, a point-to-pointer.

The most startling animal story came from 1954. In March of that year three performing bears, part of an act at the Palace Theatre, escaped from their travelling cage in Morden Street and roamed the streets of Newcastle for an hour! Women and children ran screaming and one woman was bitten on the neck by one of them. The *Chronicle's* account continued:

> They started by chasing Mr George Bell, a British Legion car park attendant, around Morden Street car park... [T]hey broke through lunch-time crowds into Percy Street. One bear raced through the Haymarket and loped past the South Africa War Memorial to the grounds of St Thomas' church. [Two police constables] saw the bear at Barras Bridge and chased it into a builder's yard at Hancock Street, where it was caught.

Charles Harris of Newcastle, a lion-tamer, c. 1910.

"PRINCE," REARED AND TRAINED BY CHARLES HARRIS, NEWCASTLE

Another scene from the circus procession, 1898.

The other bear entered Eldon Square and [got into] a basement. [Two police] officers and a civilian tried to hold a door shut and lock the bear in. The bear broke out and grabbed the civilian by the lapel. Constable Jackson came up and hit it with his cane. It released its hold and grabbed him by the trouser-leg... [I]t jumped on top of a car. [A police inspector] offered the bear a ginger snap which it took. But when he offered it a second the bear grabbed at him and chased him... [T]he bear grabbed a woman who got away but then fell and was grabbed again... Mr John Hall of Stratford Grove West... left his baker's van, fetched a thick rope and managed to loop it over the bear's head... [I]t was eventually tethered to some railings... and then taken back to its cage in a police van.

The third bear was recaptured after it chased Mr Carl Nielsen who was working in a yard adjoining the Morden Street car park.

Last night the bears put on their act as usual. 'They were just a little tired' said Hans Petersen, their Norwegian owner.

It does not appear to me that these bears were in distress whilst at large in the town. I would go further and guess that their lives as performers did not make them miserable either. Depression in bears is easy to see and is shown by many of the bears in zoos. Like most intelligent animals, they seem to need something to do. In the wild they would be busy looking for food; in captivity, so long as they were kindly treated, their stage performances would probably have been no more taxing for them than life in the wild whilst at the same time giving them regular exercise. Cruelty could of course have been present during their training but need not have been. Everything would have depended on the intelligence and compassion of their keeper. For this reason it is probably a good thing that performing animals have been banned in this country. Certainly such animals could have had a happy life with a good keeper; equally certainly with a bad keeper they would have had no redress and been at his mercy. This, I suppose, is the reason we have laws at all; if everyone were dutiful and compassionate towards others, including other species, we should have no need of them. But that is not the case. It is a comfort for us in Newcastle to remember the RSPCA's first judgement on the town – that it had no reputation for ill-treatment of animals.

A Final Note

When I first came to live in Newcastle seventeen years ago, Grainger Street was not as smart as it is now. Grainger Town Redevelopment was about to start but the street itself was, at that time, rather run-down, with charity shops even at the 'better' end, near Grey's Monument. The splendid late Georgian buildings' upper floors were grimy inside and out and mainly deserted. But every evening there was a wonderous sight to see. Hundreds and hundreds of starlings would weave around the sky above Grainger Street, gliding lower with each circling, the music of their twittering and calling loud enough even to drown the noise of the traffic. One by one and bunch by bunch they would then settle into the window alcoves to roost for the night. I was not the only person to stand and watch the spectacle, especially dramatic if the sun was setting.

Within a few years though, the window alcoves were screened off and the scaffolding went up on the fronts of the buildings one by one. Redevelopment was under way. The starlings were quick to understand and went so rapidly, one wondered whether they had been imaginary instead of real. The irony for me is that I lived in one of the flats created by the redevelopment. I found my roost as the birds lost theirs.

Bibliography

Books

Anon, *Views of the Collieries of Northumberland and Durham with Descriptive Sketches* (1844)
Barke, Mike, 'The People of Newcastle: A Demographic History' (in Colls, R. and Lancaster, B., *Newcastle upon Tyne: A Modern History* (Phillimore; 2001)
Blackman, D.E. and others, *Animal Welfare and the Law* (Cambridge University Press; 1989)
Brand, J., *Histories and Antiquities of Newcastle upon Tyne* (London; 1789)
Cobbett, William, *Political Register 1834*
Durham County Environmental Education Curriculum Group, *Coal Mining in County Durham* (1993)
Erskine, Lord Thomas, [*A Bill Before Parliament*] on *Cruelty to Animals* (printed 1809)
Fordyce, W., *Coal and Coke Fields: Descent into a Coal Pit at Monkwearmouth* (1960)
Gale, Joan, *My Pit Pony, or, the Earl of Bedlington* (1989)
Hinde, Jon Hodgson, *Public Amusements in Newcastle* (Newcastle; 1868)
Hunting, Charles, *On The Management of Pit Ponies* (Edinburgh, Jack; 1861)
Jemsion, Joan, 'First Dog Show?' *Geordie Life* (May, 1976)
Morgan, Alan, *Bygone Lower Ouseburn* (Newcastle City Libraries)
Newcastle Borough (later City) Council, *Minutes of Council Meetings* (c. 1820-c. 1920)
Newcastle RSPCA, *Annual Reports* 1873-83, 1938, 1969, 1971
Newcastle upon Tyne Dog and Cat Shelter Information Leaflet (c. 1978)
Ritvo, Harriet *The Animal Estate* (Penguin; 1990)
Stockdale, Percival, *A Remonstrance Against Inhumanity to Animals* (Alnwick, Graham; 1802)
Windham, The Hon. W., Speech in Parliament Against Lord Erskine's Bill (1810)
Youatt, W. *The Obligation and Extent of Humanity of Brutes* (Longman; 1839)

Trade Directories

Christie's Trades Directory of Newcastle upon Tyne (1874-7)
General Trades Directory of Newcastle upon Tyne (1838)
Mitchell's Trades Directory of Newcastle (1801)
Richardson's Trades Directory of Newcastle upon Tyne (1838)
Ward's Trades Directory of Newcastle (various between 1850 and 1937)

Newspapers

Newcastle Evening Chronicle (previously *Chronicle*) issues c. 1750-1990 including records of the Dicky Bird Society

Websites

Cats Protection League, www.cats.org.uk
Newcastle Racecourse, www.newcastle-racecourse.co.uk
PDSA, www.pdsa.org.uk

Other local titles published by Tempus

Newcastle Ragged School

WENDY PRAHMS

In the towns and cities of young Queen Victoria's Britain, neglected and criminal children ran wild: then came the 'Ragged Schools'. This book follows the Newcastle Ragged School through the eighty-six years of its life, describing daily triumphs and disasters. With glimpses of Newcastle itself at the time – the quayside, the cargo ships, new railways being built – this is a fascinating exploration of Newcastle's heritage.

978 07524 4088 0

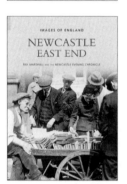

Newcastle West End

RAY MARSHALL AND THE NEWCASTLE EVENING CHRONICLE

This beautiful collection of photographs from the archives of the *Newcastle Chronicle*, compiled by Ray Marshall, the editor of the *Remember When?* section for many years, celebrates every aspect of life in the West End of the city. Many of these images have not been seen since the day they were first published 100 years ago. This fascinating record of life in the area as it used to be will delight all who know the city.

978 07524 3351 6

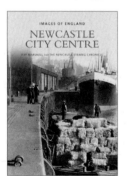

Newcastle East End

RAY MARSHALL AND THE NEWCASTLE EVENING CHRONICLE

During the eighteenth and nineteenth century the reputation of Tyneside shipbuilders spread throughout the world, and supply and support industries mushroomed. At the same time, the suburbs of Newcastle were bursting the city boundaries, and housing began to spread into new areas. All of these changes are illustrated in this beautiful collection of photographs from the archives of the *Newcastle Evening Chronicle*.

978 07524 3629 6

Newcastle City Centre

RAY MARSHALL AND THE EVENING CHRONICLE

With archive images of the building of the Tyne Bridge and the railway, bustling streets scenes, events and local characters such as 'Coffee Johnny', this is a unique tribute to life in the city. It reveals how the area, and indeed the world, has changed over the last century. Every aspect of life is here, from shoppers fighting – quite literally – to get into the January sales to workers perched on the bridge in the 1920s (without a safety harness or helmet in sight). It will delight all Tynesiders.

978 07524 3998 3

If you are interested in purchasing other books published by Tempus, or in case you have difficulty finding any Tempus books in your local bookshop, you can also place orders directly through our website

www.tempus-publishing.com